Marine Mammals

Marine Mammals

Richard J. Harrison, F.R.S.

Professor of Anatomy in the University of Cambridge

and

Judith E. King

University of New South Wales, Sydney, Australia

Hutchinson

London Melbourne Sydney Auckland Johannesburg

Hutchinson & Co. (Publishers) Ltd

An imprint of the Hutchinson Publishing Group

3 Fitzroy Square, London W1P 6JD

Hutchinson Group (Australia) Pty Ltd
30–32 Cremorne Street, Richmond South, Victoria 3121
PO Box 151, Broadway, New South Wales 2007

Hutchinson Group (NZ) Ltd
32–34 View Road, PO Box 40–086, Glenfield, Auckland 10

Hutchinson Group (SA) (Pty) Ltd
PO Box 337, Bergvlei 2012, South Africa

First published 1965
Reprinted with amendments 1968 and 1973
Second edition 1980

© R. J. Harrison and J. E. King 1965 and 1980

Printed in Great Britain by The Anchor Press Ltd
and bound by Wm Brendon & Son Ltd
both of Tiptree, Essex

ISBN 0 09 140931 4

Contents

Figures

Greatest of all is the Whale, of the beasts which live in the
waters,

Monster indeed he appears, swimming on top of the waves,

Looking at him one thinks, that there in the sea is a
mountain,

Or that an island had formed, here in the midst of the sea,

He also sometimes his hunger (which worries him often
most greatly),

Wishes at once to relieve, warm is his wide open mouth,

Whence he then sends forth breaths of odours as sweet as
the flowers.

ABBOT THEOBALDUS OF MONTE CASSINO

From *Physiologus: A Metrical Bestiary of Twelve Chapters*
c. 1022-1035

Preface

Until recently only sailors and those who lived by the sea had seen a marine mammal in its natural environment. Today with the cinema and television being widespread and with man having learnt how to maintain dolphins and seals in captivity and in circuses almost everyone has become familiar with the appearances of the commoner species. Zoologists, too, have discovered that marine mammals possess many interesting and surprising features. Recently the realization that cetaceans and seals are remarkably intelligent and are able to communicate, to swim underwater guided by a form of echo-location, and to learn, has opened up many exciting new prospects for research. This book describes the appearances of marine mammals, how they are classified, and also discusses some aspects of their anatomical and physiological adaptations to life in sea water. Some cetaceans and a few seals are very rare and little is known about them and their habits. In not a few instances classification is very difficult and is based on complex features of the skull and teeth; anyone interested further should consult the original papers, a guide to which is given in the references. Interest in marine mammals is not confined to zoologists; divers, ship designers, commercial whaling firms, furriers, circus owners and perfumiers have all learned or gained something advantageous from these animals. The products obtained from marine mammals form an important part of the economy of many groups of people besides Eskimoes and even of several countries such as Japan. The history of the development, the activities and the control of the whaling and the sealing industries are fascinating topics in themselves; sadly there is insufficient space here to do little more than mention them. Undoubtedly the pursuit of these animals has proved a stimulus to exploration and everything that follows from it. Sadly there has also often followed a decimation of a commercially useful species, of necessity leading to international control and planned conservation. Manatees and dugongs are now relatively rare animals, but their recent use as 'aquatic lawnmowers' to clear vegetation from rivers has stressed the need to protect them.

It is, however, the discovery that some cetaceans seem of all mammals to have an order of intelligence that is next to man's which is particularly exciting. Nowadays there are distinct suspicions that not all the myths and fables about their abilities are so far-fetched. Boys have indeed ridden on dolphins and it has been shown that they are playful, friendly and undoubtedly have distinct personalities. Ancient Greek writers were understandably fascinated by dolphin behaviour, though often doubting that their accounts would be accepted, and perhaps it is still the same today. W. N. Kellogg in his book on *Porpoises and Sonar* charmingly quotes Pliny the Younger on this subject: 'I have met with a story, which, although authenticated by undoubted evidence, looks very like a fable.' (*Letters* ix, 33)

We are much indebted to Professor Munro Fox, F.R.S., for encouraging us to write this book and for his helpful advice. Dr F. C. Fraser has guided us both with information and forceful comment; his friendship is much valued. We also thank Miss Barbara Fuller, who we fear may not have recovered from our views on punctuation, for preparing the manuscript and Mr Frank Price who did the drawings.

Whales, Dolphins and Porpoises

If we compare land animals in respect to magnitude, with those that take up their abode in the deep, we shall find they will appear contemptible in the comparison. The whale is doubtless the largest animal in creation.

OLIVER GOLDSMITH

There are so many surprising, unique, and still unexplainable aspects of the anatomy[2,6,8,13], physiology[2,13] and general biology[10] of cetaceans[5,11] that one is hard put to select those with which to start their description. One dramatic attribute, however, which always stuns those who see one for the first time, is the large size of the great baleen whales. The Blue Whale (*Balaenoptera musculus*) is the largest of all animals. It has been known to reach a length of 31 m and a weight of 130,000 kg. Yet this vast Leviathan is no slowcoach in the water and its diving ability is remarkable. Not all cetaceans are so enormous: Herman Melville in his famous *Moby Dick or the Whale* wrote: 'According to magnitude I divide whales into three primary BOOKS (subdivisible into Chapters and these shall comprehend them all, both small and large. I. The Folio whale; II. the Octavo whale; III. the Duodecimo whale.' Although not acceptable biologically this classification by size does remind us that there are many small cetaceans, dolphins and porpoises, some only 1·5–2·0 m in length, but among them are some of the fastest and most agile swimmers in the seas.

Cetaceans, at least modern ones, are exclusively aquatic: the majority are found in sea water, but there are several interesting fresh-water forms[11]. They are so well adapted to aquatic life that they are 'the most peculiar and aberrant of mammals. Their place in the sequence of cohorts and orders is open to question and is indeed quite impossible to deter-

mine in any purely objective way. There is no proper place
for them in a *scala naturae* or in the necessarily one-
dimensional sequence of a written classification'. This writer
argues further that cetaceans could indeed, because of
their specialization, be placed at the end of a classificatory
series. They would then, however, be far removed from any
ancestral or related forms. It would also imply that they
were the highest mammals, whereas they are really the most
atypical. Simpson[14] considers that they must be inserted into
a series in a somewhat parenthetical sense and must be
imagined to extend into a different dimension in a classificatory sense from other orders or cohorts. Cetaceans are
extremely ancient and their derivation is difficult if not
impossible to assess. At least it is probable that they arose
very early, before the lower Eocene, from a then undiffer-
entiated ancestral stock. Simpson has therefore placed the
cetaceans in a separate cohort, Mutica, a name already used
by the astute Linnaeus who nowhere displayed greater
insight and clarity than in his decisions about their place.

Towards the end of the last century enough fossil
cetaceans had been discovered for the Order to be considered
compounded of three suborders. These are the extinct
Archaeoceti, the Odontoceti or Toothed Whales and the
Mysticeti or Whalebone Whales. What is most intriguing
about the Order is the striking lack of continuous unified
phylogenetic structure and of annectent forms. There are
almost isolated, successive waves of structurally allied
forms that appear to be unrelated and whose origin can only
be surmised. The Archaeoceti[41] were undoubtedly primitive
cetaceans, already highly specialized for aquatic life, yet it
is highly unlikely that any were ancestral to the other suborders. They abounded in the middle Eocene and a few
forms persisted into the early Miocene. The first odontocetes appeared in the late Eocene and the suborder expanded
rapidly in the middle Miocene. Mysticetes appeared and
expanded later, being unknown before the middle Oligocene.
The earliest were the cetotheres, which already showed
distinctive mysticete features. What they arose from is still

conjectural, though some primitive toothed form must be a strong candidate. Kellogg[40] has written excellently on the geological and geographical distribution of cetaceans and suggests that the critical stages of their history may well have occurred locally in streams and lakes of fresh water where sediments have not persisted and in great ocean basins we have yet to explore fruitfully.

Whales have reassumed the streamlined, fusiform, torpedo-like shape of early aquatic vertebrates[8, 10, 16]. There is a shortening and even fusion of the cervical vertebrae with a consequent absence of a proper neck (Fig. 1). The body tapers gradually from the chest to the base of the tail. It is rounded in section as opposed to that of most fish. The tail is in the form of two pointed flukes, each flattened and *laterally* expanded with a concave crescentic notch on the hind edge. The plane of the flukes is thus horizontal, quite different from the vertical tail fin of a fish. The caudal vertebrae extend down the centre of the tail almost to its end, where there is sometimes a small central notch. The fluke itself is unsupported by any bones but is composed of strong connective tissue. It is the principal source of propulsive power. There is usually a dorsal fin, falcate or triangular in shape, lacking any bony support and placed somewhere near the centre of the back. The fore-limbs are modified into flippers, usually short and broad and mainly used for steering and balancing (Fig. 2). They contain the usual arrangement of limb bones, except that there are no clavicles. The scapula is fan-shaped and there may or may not be an acromion and coracoid process. The shoulder joint is of the ball and socket-variety and is synovial: yet there are hardly any cetaceans that can bend the flipper forwards beyond 90 degrees to the body axis. Humerus, radius, ulna, carpals and metacarpals are short and flattened. All the joints between these bones are fibrous and all but immovable. There are five digits except in Rorquals which lack a thumb. The digits cannot be seen within the substance of the flipper which appears externally as a smooth surfaced paddle lacking divisions into fore-arm, arm, wrist and so on.

The number of phalanges of the 2nd and 3rd digits is always more than the three found in other mammals and may be as many as fourteen in Pilot Whales (hyperphalangy). The phalanges have epiphyses at both ends. There are no nails. In cetacean foetuses the flipper exhibits transiently four grooves on its surface showing that embryonic syndactyly persists into adult life. There is no external evidence of hind limbs, but within the body just anterior to the anal opening there are two elongated slender bones sometimes with a pronounced process at the centre, enclosed in muscle. They represent the vestigial pelvis. They are not attached to the vertebral column, but do give origin to the penis in males. Occasionally one or more smaller bones are found near or fused to the larger: they are the remnants of the hind limb bones.

Cetaceans lack hair, except for a few bristles about the head in some forms. Sebaceous glands are also absent and sweat glands are much reduced or only seen in foetuses. There is a layer of blubber which varies in thickness during migration and if lactation has occurred. It is remarkably vascular (Fig. 4) and as will be shown later it has more functions than just acting as an insulating blanket. The smooth skin of cetaceans has been said to be devoid of nerve endings, but from their behaviour in captivity and from the work of several authors[6] it seems that dolphins have a very sensitive skin at least in certain regions.

The head has a shape characteristic of each main group; that of the Sperm Whale being the best known. The skull is large and heavy, with marked enlargement of the jaws to carry teeth in the odontocetes and baleen plates in the mysticetes. There is always a degree of telescoping in the cetacean skull. The maxillary bones in odontocetes have become drawn backwards over the posterior bones, often not quite equally on each side so that an interesting asymmetry is given to the skull. The most recent research suggests that it plays some part in the auditory and positioning senses of the animals when under water. The occipital bones have also become pushed forward over the top of the skull so that it has been described as being 'all front and back'. Very striking, too, is the position of the nostril, which may be single or double in the form of a 'blowhole'. It is placed on the highest point of the head well back from the snout (except in Sperm Whales where it lies near the front of the forehead). The position of the blowhole and the 'balance' of the whale in the water and the thrust derived from the horizontally placed flukes are all important in the act of respiration, particularly as it is to the creature's advantage to be able to breathe without thrusting itself unnecessarily far out of the water and to do so at speed.

The development of the huge spermaceti organ (Fig. 1) in the snout of a Sperm Whale (see p. 33) is associated with a complex arrangement of narial passages difficult to explain functionally. The caudal part of the organ projects backwards as two plugs, a small right and a larger left one. These can be pushed into the similarly unequal-sized narial tubes where they leave the bony part of the skull. The nasal passages continue forward from this point as two membraneous tubes, each having accessory diverticula (Fig. 3e). The left is the smaller and extends obliquely upwards and forwards around the spermaceti organ to reach a sac lying beneath the single blowhole near the summit of the snout. The larger right tube gives off a huge frontal sac at the point of emergence from the somewhat smaller sized bony narial aperture. This sac is very broad, but thin antero-posteriorly and lies immediately between the back of the spermaceti organ and the raised bony forehead. The right nasal tube continues forward beneath the spermaceti organ to turn upwards and open into the sac beneath the blowhole. Where it enters the sac there is a wide but strong valve, the 'monkey's muzzle' or *museau de singe*. Vestibular and premaxillary sacs are also found in relation to the passage leading to the blowhole in other odontocetes. In the Sperm Whale the complex of narial passages, diverticula, and the spermaceti organ may be involved in buoyancy[20]. When a cetacean breathes, the beak-like upper end of the larynx or glottis is raised and inserted into the back of the

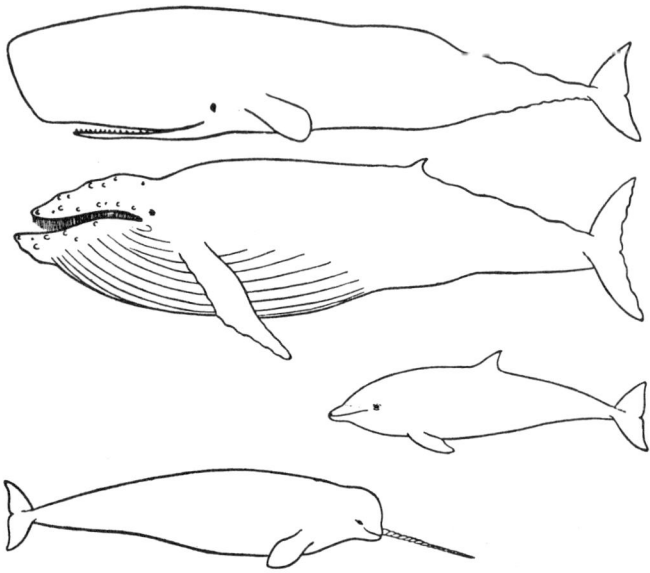

Fig. 1. Examples of living cetaceans (not to scale). From above downwards: Sperm Whale (*Physeter catodon*) 18 m long; Humpback Whale (*Megaptera novaeangliae*) 15 m long; Bottlenosed Dolphin (*Tursiops truncatus*) 3·5 m long; Narwhal (*Monodon monoceros*) 4·5 m long with tusk up to 2·5 m.

nasal cavity above the palate. It has been suggested that this enables swallowing and breathing to occur at the same time; but it is not the real explanation, for whales swallow under water when they are not breathing. It is far more likely that the mechanism enables an almost water- and air-tight connection to be made between the lungs, trachea and nasal passages with their diverticula. The opening of the blowhole in mysticetes is surrounded by elastic tissue keeping its lips together and in odontocetes there is a plug of adipose tissue that can occlude the bony narial openings. The diverticula thus become important as air reservoirs or safety valves that can help regulate the escape of air under pressure. As will be discussed later this complex narial mechanism, varying in details in different species (p. 80), may also be involved in sound production. The configuration of the blowhole, either single or double, slit-like, oval or even S-shaped, gives the spout or 'blow' of each cetacean distinct characteristics, recognizable to an expert. The blow is the result of the powerful act of expiration and consists of exhaled air containing water vapour and oily and mucous secretions from the air passages and diverticula. It is seen best in cold atmospheres but can also be seen in the tropics. The height of the blow, its type, shape and direction can all help identify the manufacturer, though better on a calm day.

Passage through water at speed will be accomplished with less effort the better the cetacean is streamlined: thus the importance of the torpedo-like body and the elongated snout. Cetaceans lack several external appendages that project outwards from the body in other mammals. There is no external pinna to the ear: the external auditory meatus presents as a small orifice on the surface midway between the edge of the eye and the base of the flipper. This in no way impairs the acuity of hearing and whales are easily frightened by strange noises. The penis is concealed beneath the abdominal skin and is protruded through a slit on the belly wall just caudal to the umbilicus. When flaccid the penis assumes an S-shaped half-coiled form beneath the abdominal skin, retractor muscles restraining it within the body. It consists of a long, rope-like corpus cavernosum, arising by two crura from the pelvic bones. The shaft can be over 3 m long and 30 cm in diameter in the largest whales. Only the anterior part is extruded, everting a fold of thin abdominal skin as it projects from the urogenital slit. Protrusion is brought about mainly by the elasticity of the shaft, partly by distension of cavernous sinuses and as a result of relaxation of the retractor muscles. The urethra lies on the ventral aspect of the front part of the shaft, surrounded by the corpus spongiosum, and ends at the pointed tip of the penis. Cetaceans lack any form of os penis or baculum such as is found in pinnipeds. They also lack a scrotum and the testes are abdominal, lying caudal and lateral to the kidneys. Intra-abdominal testes are found also in sea-cows, elephants, sloths and armadillos. It is interesting that in these forms spermatogenesis can occur quite normally within the abdomen even though the body temperature is similar to that which in other mammals renders the testes non-productive should they not descend into the scrotum. The mammary glands are also placed beneath the ventral abdominal wall extending from just caudal to the umbilicus to a little way cranial to the anus. The nipples are set in elongated recesses fairly close together on each side of the midline and a little way cranial to the anus. They become somewhat protruded at suckling which always occurs under water. The slit-like vulva is placed just in front of the anus and lacks any marked labia minora, though there may be small folds just within the entrance often related to a pronounced clitoris placed on the ventral vaginal wall.

The cetacean body form is thus beautifully adapted for swimming and apart from flippers, fin and flukes the surface is not broken by creases or folds and is well streamlined. In Rorquals and to a lesser degree in Grey Whales there is, however, a remarkable series of parallel grooves and ridges extending longitudinally on the skin beneath the chin, throat and chest almost as far as the umbilicus. They give the impression of being a series of small 'keels', but their real significance is not known. It is possible that they allow distension of the skin of the throat and chest regions during swallowing and breathing. They may also play some part in improving the Rorqual's ease of swimming by reducing 'drag', though experiments with models do not show such grooving to have much effect. More recently it has been suggested that they act as a cooling mechanism, the skin in the grooves being thinner and more vascular than that of the ridges. They thus form a sort of 'radiator' at the front of the whale.

The colour of the smooth, hairless glistening surface of whales is very variable and often its characteristics provide the only means of identifying specimens when swimming. Black and white are the predominant colours; some cetaceans are virtually either black or white all over, others display patterns of varying complexity mingled with shades of brown, pink and dark blue. Almost always, however, the animal is darkest on its dorsal surfaces and lightest ventrally. This contrasting colouration helps to camouflage the animal when seen from above and below and even when seen sideways, especially when there are also longitudinal markings or bands of contrasting colour along the flanks to blend against the breaking foam. Albino forms occur occasionally, indeed the Great White Whale, Moby Dick, written about so dramatically by Melville, was an albino Sperm Whale. There is, however, no difference in colour between sexes.

Scratches and scars, sometimes of bizarre appearance, or present as parallel stripes, are frequently seen on the skin[15]. These markings can be made by teeth of other cetaceans, by rubbing against sharp projections from ice-floes or by the suckers of squids (the giant squid *Architeuthis* can reach 12 m in length) or as a result of attacks by lampreys. Despite its smoothness the skin of cetaceans is not immune from parasites[3], predominantly sessile crustaceans which accumulate on the head, flippers and even between the teeth. Right Whales, Humpback and Sperm Whales seem to be most frequently infested, whereas the smaller dolphins and porpoises seldom carry these external parasites. Acorn **Bar-nacles** (*Coronula sp.*) are frequently seen, as also is **the** Stalked Barnacle (*Conchoderma*). The wire-like crustacean *Penella* burrows deep into the skin of Rorquals, trailing its elongated body from the surface. Whale lice (*Cyamus*) are found clinging by their appendages to the edges of **the** mouth and other orifices and are also common in old scars. An encapsulated ciliate (*Haematophagus*) and a nematode (*Odontobius*) are found living on baleen. Blue and Fin Whales often become coated on their bellies with a film of yellowish diatoms from which arose the name 'sulphur bottom' for an animal in this state.

CLASSIFICATION

Order CETACEA

Suborder ARCHAEOCETI
Families of exinct forms from the lower Eocene to upper Oligocene. Protocetidae, Dorudontidae, Basilosauridae and others such as *Patriocetus* of uncertain position.

Suborder ODONTOCETI (Toothed Whales)
Superfamily Squalodontoidea
Families Agorophiidae and Squalodontidae; extinct forms from upper Eocene to lower Pliocene.

Superfamily Platanistoidea (River Dolphins)
Family Platanistidae
Genus *Platanista*—Gangetic Dolphin, Susu
Genus *Pontoporia*—Franciscana
Genus *Inia*—Amazon River Dolphin
Genus *Lipotes*—Chinese River Dolphin

Superfamily Ziphioidea (Beaked Whales, Bottlenosed Whale)
Family Ziphiidae
    Genus *Ziphius*—Cuvier's Beaked Whale
    Genus *Mesoplodon*—Sowerby's Beaked Whale, Gray's Beaked Whale, Straptoothed Whale
    Genus *Hyperoodon*—Bottlenosed Whale
    Genus *Berardius*—Baird's and Arnoux's Beaked Whales
    Genus *Tasmacetus*—Shepherd's Beaked Whale

Superfamily Physeteroidea
  Family Physeteridae
    Genus *Physeter*—Sperm Whale
    Genus *Kogia*—Pygmy and Dwarf Sperm Whales

Superfamily Monodontoidea
  Family Monodontidae
    Genus *Monodon*—Narwhal
    Genus *Delphinapterus*—Beluga or White Whale

Superfamily Delphinoidea
  Family Stenidae
    Genus *Steno*—Rough-toothed Dolphin
    Genus *Sousa*—Hump-backed Dolphins
    Genus *Sotalia*—Tucuxi
  Family Phocoenidae
    Genus *Phocoena*—Common Porpoise
    Genus *Neophocaena*—Finless Black Porpoise
    Genus *Phocoenoides*—Dall's Porpoise
  Family Delphinidae
    Genus *Orcinus*—Killer Whale
    Genus *Pseudorca*—False Killer Whale
    Genus *Orcaella*—Irrawaddy Dolphin
    Genus *Globicephala*—Pilot Whale
    Genus *Feresa*—Slender Blackfish or Pygmy Killer
    Genus *Peponocephala*—Melon-headed Whale

Genus *Lissodelphis*—Right Whale Dolphins
Genus *Cephalorhynchus*—Commerson's
Dolphin, Heaviside's Dolphin
Genus *Lagenorhynchus*—Striped, White-beaked,
White-sided Dolphins
Genus *Lagenodelphis*—Fraser's Dolphin
Genus *Grampus*—Grampus or Risso's Dolphin
Genus *Tursiops*—Bottlenosed Dolphin
Genus *Stenella*—Spotted and Spinner Dolphins
Genus *Delphinus*—Common Dolphin

Suborder MYSTICETI
Family Cetotheriidae
Numerous extinct genera from upper Oligocene and later.
Family Balaenidae (Right Whales)
Genus *Balaena*—Greenland Right Whale
Genus *Eubalaena*—Biscayan Right Whale
Genus *Caperea*—Pygmy Right Whale
Family Eschrichtidae
Genus *Eschrichtius*—Californian Grey Whale
Family Balaenopteridae
Genus *Balaenoptera*—Rorquals. Blue, Fin, Sei,
Bryde's and Minke Whales
Genus *Megaptera*—Humpback Whale

2

Primitive Whales and Toothed Whales

The oldest and most primitive cetaceans are known as archaeocetes[10,40,41]. They appeared in the middle Eocene. Fossil remains were first found in 1832 in Alabama and Louisiana from the upper Eocene and were mistakenly thought to have been those of a reptile called *Basilosaurus* (=king of the reptiles). These remains were vertebrae, but later a skull was found and its characteristics together with those of its teeth made Richard Owen decide that it was from a mammal and he called it *Zeuglodon*, suggested by the way the roots of the posterior teeth were yoked together at the top. The situation became more complicated by the activities of a Dr Albert Koch who in 1845 dug up fossil remains which he mounted into a specimen with the name *Hydrarchos* (=water chief). He exhibited it in North America and Europe and, unaware of Owen's decision, considered it, probably because of its immense length of about 35 m, as some sort of sea snake or serpent. He had in fact included the vertebrae of at least two animals in his specimen, but even when correctly reconstructed some sixty years later it was still over 17 m long. The great length was due to an increase in the length of the centra of the individual vertebrae caudal to the mid-thoracic region and also to their increase in number caudal to the thorax. This gave great flexibility to the hinder part of what must have been very fast swimming creatures. Simpson recognizes three families of archaeocetes (Protocetidae, Dorundontidae and Basilosauridae) with another four genera as *incertae sedis*.

The oldest archaeocete is probably *Pappocetus lugardi* from Southern Nigeria. Certain features, such as those of the molar teeth, recall characters found in the early land-living carnivores, the creodonts. Another member of the Protocetidae, *Protocetus*, from the middle Eocene in Egypt had an elongated snout and showed some backward migration of the nostrils, but there was no telescoping of the skull. The dentition was primitive, with the usual placental number of forty-four, and cheek teeth were also like those of creodonts, but some other features were distinctly cetacean. Other fossil remains have been recovered from North America, Europe, New Zealand and the Antarctic but all the large, sinuous forms appear to have died out by the lower Oligocene. It has been suggested that all had horizontal flukes, though not pronounced, and short, fin-like fore flippers that had a movable elbow joint. Hind limbs seem to have been lacking though pelvic bones of larger size than in living cetaceans were present, as was a ball and socket hip-joint and a femur. There were some archaeocetes (*Dorudon*) that were shorter than the sea-serpent types, that had a torpedo-like body form and may well have resembled modern dolphins. They persisted longer, but were extinct by the beginning of the Miocene.

Were the archaeocetes precursors of modern cetaceans? They have been considered a highly specialized group that could not have been cetacean ancestors and that their cetacean features were the result of convergence or of parallel evolution. Some authorities, including Fraas, are of the opinion, however, that *Protocetus* was intermediate between creodonts and cetaceans though the divergence of the archaeocete stock from the terrestrial creodonts must have occurred in the lower Eocene. It can also be argued that the morphology of the archaeocete skull provides a possible pattern from which, by divergent paths perhaps through a form such as *Archaeodelphis*, were derived both the odontocetes and the mysticetes. There are certain objections to maintaining that there was a common origin of the two suborders[40,58], mainly on the grounds of differences in skull morphology and in particular in those of the maxilla and supraoccipital. The question as to the precise part played by the archaeocetes and whether modern cetaceans had a common ancestor must, therefore, remain unanswered until more fossil material is found. Some workers, however, have pronounced views on the problem[58].

SUBORDER ODONTOCETI: TOOTHED WHALES

This suborder comprises the great majority of living cetaceans[7]. They lack the baleen plates of the mysticetes and although called Toothed Whales, the teeth are not always obvious and the range in number is considerable. Female Beaked Whales are virtually toothless, the Narwhal has only one much enlarged tusk-like tooth, but some porpoises have as many as 300 similar conical teeth. The teeth in fact usually surpass the typical placental number of forty-four, they are peg- or wedge-shaped and are homodont.

The Cetacean skull[4] is probably one of the most modified amongst the Mammalia. The globular cranium and elongated beak or rostrum give the typical odontocete its characteristic form, although it sometimes happens that skulls of the small Common Porpoise are found on the beach and are mistakenly thought to be from large birds. It is really the position of the nares that modifies the skull. They are bounded in the normal manner by the premaxillae and nasals, but their position so far back in the skull means that the premaxillae are elongated, and contribute to the rostrum, while the nasals are only bony nodules. The asymmetry of the nares is evident, and the right premaxilla extends farther caudally than the left. The bony nasal passage is almost vertical, and there are no turbinals. The maxillae form most of the rest of the visible portion of the rostrum, and their posterior ends are expanded so that they form a large part of the dorsal surface of the skull. They lie on top of the frontals, the latter being visible dorsally only as a narrow bridge between the maxillae and supraoccipitals. The very large supraoccipital forms the back of the cranium, while the sides are formed chiefly by the

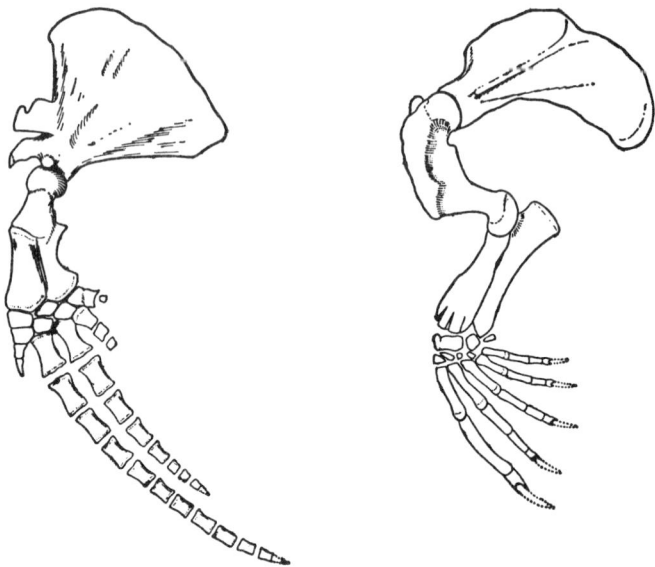

Fig. 2. Skeleton of the flippers of a Pilot Whale (left) and a seal (right). After Howell[8]

parietals which do not meet each other mid-dorsally in the normal way. The poorly defined orbits are roofed over by the flattened, plate-like frontals, and, lying immediately dorsal to these, the maxillae. The zygomatic arch is extremely slender and often broken. On the ventral surface the pterygoids are approximated, forming a continuation of the bony palate. They and the sculpturing of the ventral surface of the cranium show in the various genera increasing specialization with the development of the middle ear air sinuses. The tympanic and periotic bones are connected with the skull only by soft tissue and are frequently missing in prepared specimens. Each half of the lower jaw is nearly straight, tapering to the symphysis; the posterior end is expanded and fragile, the coronoid and articulating processes are small.

The cervical vertebrae are compressed, disc-like bones, showing varying degrees of fusion according to the species. The centra of the other vertebrae are slightly shortened, but the neural spines and transverse processes are very long, giving attachment to those muscles used in locomotion. The spinous processes and the articulations gradually diminish towards the tail, as the need for greater flexibility increases, and there is an increase in the number of lumbar vertebrae. There are no obvious sacral vertebrae, but the caudal vertebrae are marked by the V-shaped chevron bones on their ventral surfaces[6]. The pelvis is represented by two small rod-like bones. The ribs are long and slender. The anterior ones have two heads, but with the increase in size of the transverse processes it is impossible for the posterior ribs to retain any articulation with the centra. The scapula is fan-shaped, and both acromion and coracoid project forwards from the anterior edge. The humerus is very short, its rounded head articulating with the scapula, but there is no movement between the rest of the bones of the flipper. The radius and ulna are short and flattened, and the carpal bones are polygonal and fit closely together. Five digits are normally present, although the first is rudimentary. The phalanges are flattened, rectangular bones, whose number may be greatly increased, particularly those of the second digit. This leads to a long, narrow flipper: its greatest development is in the Pilot Whale (Fig. 2) where there may be as many as fourteen phalanges in the second digit. The flipper is free from the body from about the level of the radius. There is no indication of nails or claws.

The most primitive odontocetes known are the Agorophiidae, a group which Simpson considers may be ancestral to all other odontocetes. They are from the upper Eocene in North America. Nothing is known of their skeletons, but they show some telescoping in their skulls (*Agorophius*) and the nostrils are far back above the orbits. The next forms are the Squalodontidae which appeared first in the late Oligocene and which are probably derived from a type like *Agorophius*. They are called squalodonts because of their triangular shark-like teeth. They flourished to become world wide in the early Miocene: in size and shape and probably habits they resembled modern dolphins. Many had long snouts and the number of teeth reached over 180. The telescoping of the skull is complete and the blowhole is found above and behind the eyes. There is, however, little or no asymmetry of the skull. Squalodonts did not survive long, one form only is found in the Pliocene, and even by the middle Miocene other porpoise-like types had replaced them. Simpson considers them well divorced from any possible line of ancestry for the contemporaneous and later types of odontocetes. The forms of living cetaceans closest to the squalodonts are perhaps the platanistoids or River Dolphins of South America and China. The teeth are not really of squalodont type, being conical, but there are primitive features such as the still unroofed temporal opening.

FAMILY PLATANISTIDAE: RIVER DOLPHINS

The living members[11] of this family (Superfamily Platanistoidea), comprising four genera, are all fresh-water River Dolphins, though it is fairly certain that their ancestors, of which some presumed fossil remains are known from the Pliocene, lived in the sea. One fossil form (*Pachyacanthus*) even survived into the middle Miocene. The skull is not so telescoped as in higher cetaceans and the individual bones are more easily recognizable. The jaws are very slender and elongated, the two sides of the lower jaw lying close together for much of its length. The cervical vertebrae are large and separate. Eight pairs of ribs, double-headed, are usually present and also a large sternum.

The Gangetic Dolphin or Susu (*Platanista gangetica*) is about 1·7–2·0 m long. The name Susu comes from the noise it makes when breathing. The animal was known to Pliny who gave it the name *Platanista*. Its elongated forceps-like beak bears slender pointed teeth, so long at the tip of the snout that they are easily visible when the mouth is shut, and interlocking so finely that they make a formidable instrument. The forehead rises abruptly and the blowhole is a longitudinal slit on the top of the head, differing in its shape from that in other members of the group. The dorsal fin is a low, flattened triangle set two-thirds of the way down the back. The flippers are short but very broad and scalloped at their extremities. The skull is distinguished by two flanges of bone projecting forwards from the maxillary region and nearly meeting anterior to the nasal passage. This feature, together with the marked elongation of the beak and the fifty or more closely set teeth in each jaw, make the skull unique among those of living cetaceans. The body colouration is dark black all over. The dolphin is found only in the Ganges and Bramaputra (and *P.indi* in the Indus) where it feeds on fishes and fresh-water crustaceans. It uses its beak to stir them out of the mud and as it is virtually blind this structure is functionally important. The small eye is said to be without a lens and the optic nerve and eye muscles are poorly developed: the dolphin is active at night. The brain is relatively smaller than that of other dolphins of similar size and the cerebral cortex has few convolutions. The cerebellum, however, appears to be large and well developed. The kidneys are reported to be less lobulated and smaller than those of a sea-living porpoise of even smaller body size, features which may be associated with the Gangetic Dolphin's fresh-water environment.

The Amazon River Dolphin or Boutu (*Inia geoffrensis*) is another fresh-water plantanistid some 2·0–2·5 m long found only in the upper Amazon (see also *Sotalia*, p. 40). It also has a long beak, but with some bristles on it, a rare example of a hair-bearing cetacean. The conical teeth number over 120. The flippers are large and fan-shaped and the flukes relatively larger than would seem necessary, a modification possibly for the swift swimming in fresh water these dolphins are said to be able to achieve. Body colour is variable from black with pink or even a creamy pink tone ventrally. The dolphins usually keep company, two or up to six together. The optic retrogression is not as extreme as in the Gangetic Dolphin, perhaps associated with the clearer water of the Amazon. The pale brown Franciscana (*Pontoporia blainvillei*) is a shorter form, seldom more than 1·6 m long, from the estuary of the River Plate. It is probably the most specialized of the River Dolphins from the point of view of its skeletal structure. The blowhole is crescentic, as it is in the Boutu. The Chinese River or White Flag Dolphin (*Lipotes vexillifer*) is found in the Tung Ting Lake and near its mouth, some 600 miles up the Yangtze Kiang River. It is grey on the back, white below and is about 2·2 m long. The beak is a foot long and upcurved. The dorsal fin is a little more marked than in other platanistids and the flipper is broad and blunt. The blowhole is nearly rectangular.

FAMILY ZIPHIIDAE

Included in this family are the Beaked Whales[10,11], forms of which first appeared in the early Miocene as small dolphin-like creatures (*Notocetus*) which resembled squalodonts in some respects, such as their teeth. During the Miocene primitive ziphioid forms appeared (*Choneziphius*) which displayed the characteristically reduced dentition of modern

Beaked Whales. Early Sperm Whales (see Physeteridae, p. 33), small and resembling primitive porpoises, arose in the Miocene as well. They still retained teeth in the upper jaw, but their skull showed some evidence of the development of a pocket for the large oil reservoir.

The Beaked and Bottlenosed Whales reach a length of from 5–13 m. Their skulls have the region behind the nasal apertures set very high, the posterior edges of the maxillae curving down on either side as a sharp edged crest. A marked rostrum and small oil reservoirs are present. Two diverging grooves run backwards in the skin under the throat. The flippers are small and the dorsal fin is set well back on the body. Young animals appear toothless, but later a pair of teeth at least appear in the lower jaw, but only in males. Rows of very small vestigial teeth are often found in both upper and lower jaws; they resemble to some extent those of ancestral dolphin-like forms. There is a single crescentic blowhole. The stomach is divided into several compartments. The intestine is shorter than in other cetaceans, but its internal lining is elaborately folded.

The abundant northern Bottlenosed Whale (*Hyperoodon ampullatus*) is better known than the southern form (*H. planifrons*). The distinct bulging forehead of this animal, which increases with age, distinguishes it from other ziphioids. As well as the usual ziphioid elevation of the bones behind the nares, *Hyperoodon* is characterized by the enormous development of the rostral parts of the maxillae in front of the nares to form two closely approximated bosses of bone which may in old animals be the highest point of the skull and which underlie the 'forehead'. An oil reservoir is present in the melon and accounts for the whale being hunted in Arctic waters in the late 1800's before Rorqual killing began. A pair of large conical teeth is present at the tip of the lower jaw, but only in adults do their tips erupt beyond the gum. Cuttle-fish are their main food. The body colour is dark grey to black above and grey to white below. Individuals are frequently seen off British coasts (males reach 10 m and females 8 m) and

65 became stranded between 1913 and 1966: usually these are whales migrating southward[28].

Cuvier's Beaked Whale (*Ziphius cavirostris*) is smaller (5–6 m) than the Bottlenosed Whale and is widely distributed. Its beak is shorter and there is no pronounced forehead. Only in males do the single pair of conical teeth erupt at the tip of the lower jaw. It is difficult to distinguish this form, except by its cranial characteristics. Thirty have stranded[28] on British coasts since 1913. Not much is known of the two species in the genus *Berardius*, Baird's and Arnoux's Beaked Whales. *B. bairdi* comes from the north Pacific and *B. arnuxi* from southern waters off New Zealand and the Falkland Islands. Both forms are like *Hyperoodon* but the rostral bosses are not so large and there are four large, compressed, roughly triangular teeth in the lower jaws, the larger pair being at the tip of the jaw. *B. bairdi* is the largest ziphioid known and may reach over 13 m in length.

Some twelve species are included in the genus *Mesoplodon*, the name of which means that its members are armed with a tooth in the middle of the jaw. Not all of them in fact have teeth in this position, but the position and shape of the single pair of often large teeth in the lower jaw are useful distinguishing criteria, although to make things even more difficult, the teeth usually do not erupt in females. Most of the species are very rare: the commonest is Sowerby's Whale (*M. bidens*) but several species are represented only by two or a few more specimens and more information will probably reduce the number of species.

Sowerby's Whale reaches a length of 5 m. It is a not uncommon north Atlantic form and a few have been stranded on British coasts. One was kept alive out of water for a day or so in a French port in 1828. It was said to have made a noise like a cow: the animal has been known as 'cow-fish'. Its shape is more slender and tapering than in other ziphioids but mostly it has a typical beaked-whale appearance. The tooth in each half of the lower jaw is about one-third of the way back from the front and is triangular in outline. The only other species of *Mesoplodon* to be stranded on British coasts is True's Beaked Whale (*M. mirus*) and it has been recorded only three times. The very rare Gervais' Beaked Whale (*M. europaeus*) has been once found dead in the English Channel: and even after about 120 years it is known only from less than a dozen specimens mainly from the Gulf Stream coast of east America. Even from a brief description of this genus it will be realized that much is still to be learnt about its members, particularly on their distribution. They are an interesting group, perhaps particularly so from an odontological aspect, their reduced dentition and the odd positioning of the two teeth that erupt, as well as other characteristics, making them almost aberrant among cetaceans. Perhaps the most peculiar in this respect is the Straptoothed Whale (*M. layardi*). The single pair of flattened, ribbon-like teeth grow longer with age, curving over the upper jaw and eventually preventing the mouth from opening more than a limited amount. To complete the Beaked Whales it is necessary to mention *Tasmacetus shepherdi*, described in 1937, and known first from a single animal washed ashore in New Zealand and from only seven other specimens. Although undoubtedly ziphioid, it differs from all others in the number of conical functional teeth. It has fifty-two teeth in the lower jaws, with a pair of large bulbous teeth at the tip, and thirty-eight in the upper jaws.

FAMILY PHYSETERIDAE

Three representatives are placed in this family, the Sperm, the Pygmy Sperm and the Dwarf Sperm Whale. All possess a characteristic spermaceti organ, but in the Sperm Whale it gives the head a dramatic shape that is probably one of the best known amongst all whales. The upper jaws are slender and depressed, but behind them the skull rises to a great transverse crest moulded into a concave basin with high edges to receive the spermaceti organ. The ascending processes of the maxillae are also expanded to support the convex under surface of the oil sac. The blowhole is single and placed on the left side near the front end of the head. The asymmetrical distortion of the skull about the blowhole is very marked in both forms, and the right premaxilla is expanded backward. The upper jaw lacks functioning teeth, only vestiges of tooth germs remain in the gums. The lower jaw, however, retains a well-developed series of large conical teeth ranging from sixteen to thirty in each half-jaw. They are some 20 cm long and are set in deep bony sockets. When the jaws close the teeth occlude into recesses lined by fibrous tissue in the upper jaw. The cervical vertebrae are fused together except the atlas which remains mobile.

The massive head of the Sperm Whale[56] or Cachalot (*Physeter catodon*) makes it easily recognizable even at a great distance (Fig. 1). The head accounts for about a third of its 20 m adult male length and the front is occupied above by an oil reservoir (the 'case', containing clear spermaceti oil) and below by a mass of fibrous and elastic tissue with oil in its interstices (the 'junk'). 'Sperm' is a contraction of spermaceti, which solidifies on exposure to air and cold into a wax that can be used for making candles and cosmetics. It is a much more complex mixture than usually stated: it consists of cetyl esters of lauric and myristic acid, but esters of palmitic, stearic and caprinic acid are also present. The head is not really as cuboid as might seem, the front is almost vertical to the long axis but the sides have longitudinal depressions and the underside of the head is narrow and keeled. The lower jaw does not reach as far as the front of the head and gives the creature a rather odd and characteristic appearance as if its mandible had not grown properly. There is no true dorsal fin, instead a series of low ridges are present on the caudal third of the back; the front one, the largest, was called the 'hump' by the old open boat whalers. The body of the older animals is irregularly corrugated and there are short poorly defined furrows beneath the throat. The flippers are broad and paddle-like, but surprisingly small for so large an animal. The tail flukes are broad, often over 4 m across and the hinder margin has a notch in the middle. There is a striking difference in the size of the females, they are hardly ever more than half the length of the males. The colour is a dark bluish grey with a gradual lightening on the flanks and light grey or white on the belly. Some specimens may even become pie-bald, and often white scars and circles are seen in the head region. These are the result of fights with the giant cuttle-fish which form the main food of Sperm Whales, though they do eat fish as well, including sharks on occasion. It is possible, at least anatomically, for a Sperm Whale to swallow a man, but there is no authentic record of one having done so (it is said to have happened in a whaling story and perhaps to Jonah!).

Sperm Whales are found in all the oceans of the world but it is almost exclusively the old males which swim into higher, colder latitudes. A few strandings have occurred on British coasts. Sperm Whales are polygamous and the younger bulls drive off older males to obtain leadership of the herds. Occasional aggressive rogue-males break away from the herds and lead an independent existence (for example Moby Dick). Fights among males at the mating season are another cause of the scars on the skin. The largest concentrations of Sperm Whales are found off the coasts of Peru and off the Galapagos Islands, where the cool northward flowing Humboldt current mixes with equatorial waters and where cuttle-fish are abundant.

Sperm Whales are great swimmers and divers. They can remain submerged for an hour and sonar shows dives as deep as 2,250 m: one indeed is believed to have broken a cable at 1,134 m. Usual swimming speed is 3 knots, but spurts of over 10 knots can be easily achieved. At the surface they breathe about six times every minute. They are also able to sleep deeply for hours near the surface, and have while asleep suffered mortal collisions with ships. The blowhole is S-shaped to some extent, and the blow is made obliquely to a height of 5–6 m. The anatomy of the air passages in Sperm Whales is described on p. 15.

Sperm Whale products are commercially important and

in several countries much use is made of them. An indication of their value is shown by the world catch of 11,977 Sperm Whales in the season 1976–7 with a sperm oil production of 370,170 barrels. Case oil is mixed with blubber oil and six barrels of whale oil weigh one ton. In general 30·9 barrels of oil are obtained from a large whale and the oil has fetched up to £470 per ton, though the value varies depending on a number of economic factors. From 1,600 sperms caught by Japanese whalers in the north Pacific and Bering Sea in 1959 the following products were obtained: 74,471 barrels of oil, 96·6 tons of meat meal, 49·5 tons of liver oil, 2,498 tons of frozen meat, 17·5 tons of meat extract, 253·5 tons of tail flukes, 303·9 tons of gelatine materials and 433·8 tons of other products. The liver is an excellent source of Vitamin A. Sperm oil was used to make candles, now it is used in the manufacture of cosmetics. Spermaceti can be used in ointments readily absorbed by human skin. It is a good lubricant, especially for certain engines. It has also been included in detergents and boot polish. The meat is edible and it is also turned into soup cubes and cattle food. Bones can be turned into glue and gelatin, films, jellies and sweets. The teeth can be elaborately and beautifully carved into statuettes, chess men and buttons (scrimshaw work). In Japan parts of the skin are used to make leather goods. From the intestines of Sperm Whales, and from them alone, ambergris is obtained. This substance is formed as a concretion in the gut and may be collected there or found floating in the sea. It is blackish or brownish grey, looks like dried tar or bark and has an offensive odour when fresh from the animal, but eventually acquires an earthy, musk-like smell. It consists of a complex aliphatic alcohol and certain oily substances not yet identified. When dried it is not pliable and not at all sticky, but dissolves in many organic solvents. Cuttle-fish beaks are often embedded in the masses, which may sometimes weigh over 450 kg. Its cause and the mechanism of its formation are unknown, but it would seem to be an abnormal product, perhaps the result of cuttle-fish beaks causing reactions in the intestinal contents and secretions. Ambergris is still used in the higher quality products in the perfume industry, not so much for its own scent, but for its quality of retaining the odour of refined and expensive perfumes. It used to be as valuable as gold, but the price is now between £2 and £5 per ounce, there being many synthetic substitutes.

The Pygmy Sperm Whale (*Kogia breviceps*) is only 2·7–3·4 m long and its head is only one-sixth of the total length. Its Latin name indicates that it is a 'short-headed codger'. It resembles its larger relative but is more porpoise-like in form. It has a shortened lower jaw. There is a small dorsal fin and no 'humps'. The flipper is tapered. The colour is black with light grey below. It is not common and appears to eat small cuttle-fish and crabs. Widely distributed it has been stranded on French and Dutch coasts, and once on Co. Clare in 1966. A small spermaceti case is present. The small Dwarf Sperm Whale (2·1–2·7 m), *Kogia simus*, is mainly tropical and has fewer mandibular teeth.

FAMILY MONODONTIDAE

Only two species are included in this family, though both display sufficient features to merit their separation from the other families. They are the Narwhal (Fig. 1), a word of Scandinavian origin perhaps alluding to the greyish death-like colour (*nar*, a corpse), and the White Whale. The tusk of the Narwhal (*Monodon monoceros*) is well known in its association with the origin of the 'unicorn', an imaginary animal with cloven feet, yet a horse-like body, a tail of a lion and a single horn sprouting from its forehead. Queen Elizabeth I is said to have considered its horn one of her most valuable possessions and it was thought to be endowed with mystical medicinal properties. It was realized in the seventeenth century that the horn was really the incisor tusk of the Narwhal. The tusk is usually present only on the left side of males, though occasionally a right one erupts as well: females lack the tusks, which fail to erupt.

The body is 5 m long in adult males, the tusk projects up to a further 2·8 m. It is characteristically spiralled (anticlockwise looked at from the animal's point of view), even if there are two tusks present. There are no other teeth, though unerupted ones can be found in foetuses, and Narwhals catch their prey, crustaceans, cuttle-fish and fish, with their toughened jaw edges and then swallow it. The function of the tusk is something of a mystery: it may simply be a secondary sexual characteristic or it might act as an appendage for searching out food. The pulp cavity runs almost throughout the length of the tusk and it would be interesting to know if there were a plentiful innervation of the pulp. Narwhals do not use the tusk for fighting; if it gets broken it is a severe disability as the pulp gets easily infected. Odontocetes exhibit variable degrees of asymmetry of the skull and that of the Narwhal is very marked. It is tempting to associate this asymmetry with the huge tusk, though there may be another significance in connection with 'position sense' below the water (see p. 79).

The Narwhal has a rounded head, there is a low ridge about 3–5 cm high along the back in place of a dorsal fin. Adults are variably mottled on the back with dark greyish blotches on a white-grey background. It is found only in Arctic waters and is said to appear in small herds of the same sex. Even though Narwhals can swim powerfully they are much hunted. Eskimoes prize them for the tusks and their blubber which gives a reasonable oil.

The White Whale (*Delphinapterus leucas*) or Beluga[70] (a Russian word) is close to the Narwhal and would be quite like one with its tusks removed. It is circumpolar in distribution and is abundant in the Gulf of St Lawrence and in the White Sea. It is a rare visitor to British waters and has only occasionally become stranded on our coasts, the last time being in 1932 near the Forth Bridge. It was displayed twice in London in the late 1870's, though transport problems were not easy from Labrador and Newfoundland, and later often in American and British oceanaria. The White Whale lacks a dorsal fin but has a reasonably defined neck that differentiates it from most cetaceans. Both jaws possess teeth, up to ten in each half-jaw, that may have accessory cusps. The skin changes from grey to white as the animals mature and adults lack any markings or mottled patches, a striking characteristic. Specimens longer than 5 m have seldom been reported.

SUPERFAMILY DELPHINOIDEA

This comprises the three interesting families, the Stenidae or little known Long-beaked Dolphins, the Phocaenidae or porpoises, and the Delphinidae or dolphins in the stricter sense: much more is known about the last two families although there are many rare forms and quite a number of classificatory difficulties about several genera[7]. Although all are really either dolphins or porpoises, in popular language the larger ones are called 'whales'. Most are less than 5 m in length, but there are some larger forms such as the Pilot Whale. The dolphins (in the stricter sense) are the most numerous and there are fourteen modern genera. They probably developed rapidly out of the primitive toothed whale stock (primitive Squalodontidae). Even in the early Miocene when squalodonts flourished there were many 'dolphins' in existence that showed modern features. One of the commonest forms was *Eurhinodelphis* with its very elongated rostrum. Another, that appeared in the late Miocene and Pliocene was *Kentriodon* which, with its numerous modern characteristics, may well have been a form similar to the ancestors of the porpoises and dolphins.

FAMILY STENIDAE

The Rough-toothed or Spinner Dolphin (*Steno bredanensis*) is found in the warmer parts of the Indian and Atlantic Ocean. It resembles the Common Dolphin in shape and size but differs from it in the length of the jaw, its furrowed and larger teeth, and by the colour and markings on its back. It grows to 2·8 m. The genus *Sotalia* is now considered to comprise only one species, *S. fluviatilis*, called the Tucuxi from the Amazon, but there are two populations, a river and a marine, found off South American coasts. *S. guianensis, S. pallida, S. tucuxi* and *S. brasiliensis* have been described but need further study[59]. All are small, up to 1·5 m. Hump-backed Dolphins are included in the genus *Sousa* which also needs revision. They are found in the eastern tropical Atlantic and the Indo-Pacific. *S. teuszii* is about 2·7 m long and is found in rivers in Senegal and the Cameroons. All have a dorsal hump behind the fin. Probably the whitest of all cetaceans is the Indo-Pacific Hump-backed (Chinese White) Dolphin (*S. sinensis*) but little is known about it.

FAMILY PHOCAENIDAE (PORPOISES)

The Common Porpoise (*Phocoena phocoena*) was plentiful off the coasts of north Atlantic, the North Sea, the Baltic and the White Sea. It explores far up rivers, and has entered the Mediterranean but pollution has affected numbers.

The differences between porpoises and dolphins are confusing to people who are not zoologists (and even to many who are). The situation is made worse by Americans calling the Bottlenosed Dolphins, and other dolphins 'porpoises'. The porpoises are in fact easily distinguished: they are small 'tubby' cetaceans that *lack* a projecting beak, have a triangular dorsal fin, oval and relatively small flippers and twenty-three pairs of spade-like as opposed to conical teeth in both jaws.

Common Porpoises have a black back and white belly: they are seldom more than 2 m long. They are active animals and fast swimmers, even so they are the most commonly stranded cetacean off British coasts[28] (631 in 53 years) and many get entangled and drowned in nets. In our experience of many dozen animals acquired in such ways all were unhealthy, having massive infestations of worms and flukes in both respiratory and alimentary systems. They can jump clear of the water, but they cannot tolerate being removed from it for long. They are exceedingly timid and very difficult to catch alive. They were a popular delicacy for the table in medieval times.

There are several other porpoises beside the Common form, but they are rare or very rare indeed. There is Burmeister's Porpoise (*P. spinipinnis*) of South America and the Spectacled Porpoise (*P. dioptrica*) also of South America, and the cochito (*P. sinus*) from the Gulf of California. Dall's Porpoise (*Phocoenoides dalli*) is in a separate genus. All are small, but have characteristic differences in colour, fins, number of teeth and other features. In a separate genus is the more abundant Finless Black Porpoise (*Neophocaena phocaenoides*) of Indian and Chinese coasts, which may have two geographic forms.

FAMILY DELPHINIDAE

This family is nowadays divided into four subfamilies: the Orcinae, including Killer, False Killer and Pilot Whales; the Lissodelphinae or Right Whale Dolphins; the Cephalorhynchinae including Commerson's and other relatively rare dolphins of southern waters; and the Delphininae which includes the Common and Bottlenosed Dolphins. The better known species are described below.

The Killer Whale (*Orcinus orca*), also called the Grampus, has a reputation for ferocity unequalled among cetaceans and has attacked and eaten large whales, dolphins, porpoises, seals, penguins, fish and squid. Killer whales usually hunt in packs from as few as three to as many as forty or more. There are many remarkable stories about their activities when hunting, how they attack together and how they can dislodge their prey from an ice floe by tipping it from below. They even attack recently killed whales being towed to the factory ship. They tear large prey, such as a seal, into big pieces, swallow small animals whole, and there is a record of the remnants of 27 porpoises and seals in one stomach[24]. When hunting in packs they attack large whales by seizing them by the flukes, lips and tongue.

Killer whales are world-wide in distribution, but are more plentiful in polar waters. They have been washed up on British coasts forty times in the last fifty years. The adult males reach a length of 10 m, but the females only reach some 6–8 m, one of the few examples of females being smaller. The colouration is black with several distinctive white areas on the belly, below the chin, above and behind the eye and on the flank behind the dorsal fin. The fin is striking in old male animals in that it is vertically triangular and may reach a height of up to 2 m. The flippers, which are rounded and not pointed, and the tail flukes also enlarge disproportionately in old males. The shape of the animal reflects its speed and power and its jaws indicate that it is a formidable predator. There is no beak and the dorsal curvature of the front of the animal is in a smooth convex sweep backwards. There are twenty teeth in both upper and lower jaws. They are large, oval in section and about 2·5 cm in diameter, implanted in strong sockets and interlocking when the jaws close.

Although closely related to the Killer, the False Killer Whale (*Pseudorca crassidens*) has several external differences; it has even been confused with the Pilot Whale. It is not such a large animal as the Killer, and is more slightly built, seldom reaching more than 5 m in length; the males do not grow much larger than the females. It lacks a beak, though its snout projects beyond the tip of the lower jaw. The dorsal fin is small and recurved. The flippers are elongated and tapered, unlike the rounded ones of *Orcinus* and shorter than those of *Globicephala*. The colour is black almost all over.

False Killer Whales are deep water, oceanic forms and apparently not at all at home in coastal waters, estuaries or sandy bays. They are almost world-wide in distribution[5,11], and it is their sporadic and widely separated strandings that suggests they are pelagic. They are gregarious, thus strandings usually involve up to several hundred individuals of both sexes and of various ages. It has been suggested that changes in ocean currents could cause alterations in the distribution of squid, cod and other fishes on which they feed, so bringing them to coastal waters. The False Killer does not share any of the vicious reputation of the Killer. Its teeth, too, are not quite so formidable, even if they are large for the size of the animal. There are twenty conical teeth, circular in cross-section, in each jaw.

The Irrawaddy Dolphin (*Orcaella brevirostris*) is another of the Delphinidae that lacks a beak. It is a small dolphin, about 2·3 m in length, with a rather plump forehead. There is some indication of a surface indentation where the neck is. The dorsal fin is small and hook-like: the flippers are longish and triangular. It is slate-blue in colour and lacks distinctive markings. The teeth are small, conical and vary between twenty and forty in total number, sometimes unequally distributed in the four half-jaws. There is some doubt as to whether there is one or two species, but at least there is one river form found over 900 miles upriver in the Irrawaddy and another in the Bay of Bengal and off Indo-China. Local fishermen believe that the dolphins can help them by guiding fish into their nets.

The Long-finned Pilot Whale (*Globicephala melaena*), also called the Ca'aing Whale, lives in the north Atlantic and is common in waters off the Faroes, Orkney and Shetlands. They are often seen off the north-east coasts of Scotland, particularly on calm, summer evenings. They swim in herds, up to several hundred in strength and there is evidence that they migrate. The body is black, with a white splodge beneath the chin. The head bulges conspicuously, the flippers are long and narrow and there are ten teeth on each side of both jaws. The adults are about 8 m in length, but may be even longer. The herds are easily alarmed and can be driven ashore by men in boats. Meat from stranded and driven animals was of great value to Faroe Islanders.

G. scammoni is found in the north Pacific, but may be a sub-species of *G. macrorhynchus* which is more widely distributed. They are all much like *G. melaena*, but with some skull and fin differences. Despite their apparent nervousness, Pilot Whales have been captured alive and transferred to oceanaria. They have been trained[13]: they have, however, a somewhat alarming tendency when on heat to make advances to divers feeding them.

The slender Blackfish (*Feresa attenuata*), also called the Pygmy Killer, was first recognized in 1827, and again in 1875, on both occasions from skulls without localities. It was not until 1952 that another animal, painstakingly reconstructed after being caught and flensed off Taiji, Japan, yielded the first account of its external appearance. This was an old female, about 2·3 m long, dark grey all over but with white lips and a white area in the anal region. The head is rounded, with no beak, and the teeth are rather large, with ten to thirteen in each half-jaw. Another was captured at Yenn, Senegal, in 1958, but only the skull could be saved. Recently a few more have been caught off Japan, and they have been kept in captivity in Hawaii and Japan.

The two species in the genus of Right Whale Dolphins (*Lissodelphis*) lack a dorsal fin like the Right Whale (*Balaena*) They are 2·0–2·7 m long with a slender tapering form and a distinct, but short beak. *L. peroni* is found in the southern seas and is easily recognized by its black back and white lower half. *L. borealis* of the north Pacific is more generally pigmented.

The dolphins included in the genus *Cephalorhynchus* are small, porpoise-like and with a strikingly marked colouration, none more so than Commerson's Dolphin (*C. commersoni*) which seems in the water to be two black ends with white between and may thus be well camouflaged. It has been called Le Jacobite or the Piebald 'porpoise'. All are found in southern seas and none is common. The Black Dolphin (*C. eutropia*) from South America is probably the rarest, but little is known of many members of the group. Heaviside's Dolphin is seen off the Cape of Good Hope and Hector's Dolphin off New Zealand. They have a triangular dorsal fin and not much of a beak.

have a triangular dorsal fin and not much of a beak.

The forms in the genus *Lagenorhynchus* have a short, rather poorly marked beak (flask-shaped snout), a high dorsal fin with a concave posterior border, marked ridges behind the fin and anus and quite powerful flippers with pointed tips. As with other forms of dolphin there are numerous distinguishing features in the skull, teeth and skeleton: the number of vertebrae, for example, can be as many as ninety. There are often quite marked colour distinctions as well, particularly on the flanks.

Six species are now recognized; others with nostalgic names such as Wilson's Hour-glass Dolphin (*L. wilsoni*) and Fitzroy's Dolphin (*L. fitzroyi*) are of historical interest only, and actually were one of the six forms known today. The former was seen by Antarctic expeditions, the second was obtained by the *Beagle* off Patagonia, was measured by Charles Darwin and called after Captain Fitzroy who also made a drawing of it. *L. cruciger*, only 2·0 m in length, with striking white bands on the flanks, is a rare species from the South Pacific and probably was Fitzroy's dolphin[7].

Peale's Dolphin (*L. australis*) is another rare form from the southern hemisphere; it is a little larger than the one mentioned above, which is one of the smaller dolphins, and is up to 2·2 m in length. Somewhat better known in southern waters is the Dusky Dolphin (*L. obscurus*): it is a common dolphin in New Zealand waters and has been displayed in that country.

Larger still are the two northern forms, the White-sided Dolphin (*L. acutus*) and the White-beaked Dolphin (*L. albirostris*). They grow to 3 m in length and their common names indicate their external features. They are gregarious and schools of as many as 1,500 have been reported. Their range in the north Atlantic extends from Greenland to as far south as Cape Cod and to British coasts where schools of twenty to thirty animals have on occasion become stranded. Their teeth are small, those of *L. acutus* being only 5 mm in diameter, but with thirty pairs in upper and lower jaws, these dolphins in their large schools can devour considerable quantities of fish, usually herrings and whiting. Very like these two forms is *L. obliquidens* of the north Pacific, which has been on display in California.

Fraser's (or Hose's) Dolphin (*Lagenodelphis hosei*) was not recognized as a separate genus until 1956, from a skull and skeleton sent to London in 1895 from the Lutang River, Baram, Borneo: the original animal was about 2 7 m long, but badly decomposed. It has been seen often since 1970 in tropical waters. The skull, in general shape, shows resemblances to *Lagenorhynchus*, but on the ventral surface of the rostrum are grooves similar to those characteristic of *Delphinus*.

Risso's Dolphin (*Grampus griseus*) is widely distributed from the north Atlantic to New Zealand (Pelorus Jack was so highly regarded it received official protection for its trips between Nelson and Wellington). It is a fairly large beakless dolphin up to 4 m long and with an almost vertical 'forehead'. The dentition is interesting in that there are usually no teeth in the upper jaw and only five or so in the front of each lower half-jaw. This dolphin is usually found alone or in very small schools. Grampus is merely an abbreviation of *grand poisson*.

The Bottlenosed Dolphin (*Tursiops truncatus*) has become the best-known of the dolphins by virtue of its popularity as a performer in oceanaria (Fig. 1). It is fairly easily captured, will soon feed in captivity and can be taught tricks[13]. A great swimmer and jumper, it seems to enjoy being put through its paces and sometimes appears to 'show-off' after accomplishing a spectacular trick. It is a large dolphin, up to 4 m long, with a short snout and slightly protruding lower jaw. A well-marked central dorsal fin has its apex curved backwards to a sharp point. The back is black to grey and the belly and lower jaw white. There are twenty pairs of teeth on both jaws. It is common off the east American coast, and it is easily caught in shallow waters off Florida for export to oceanaria overseas. It is the third most commonly stranded cetacean[28] on British coasts (185 in 53 years). Another species is claimed for the Red

Sea, Indian and Australian waters (*T. aduncus*): *T. gilli* and
T. nuuanu are other alleged species but all seem much like
T. truncatus.

Six species of Spinner and Spotted Dolphins (*Stenella*)
are now recognized[59,62]. They are distinguished by mor-
phological features of teeth and skull. The Slender Dolphin
(*S. attenuata*) is found in the warm regions of the Atlantic,
the Spotted Dolphin (*S. plagiodon*) occurs off the North
American east coast. Other species are found in the Atlantic,
Indian and Pacific Oceans (*S. longirostris*). *S. coeruleoalba*
is from temperate waters. It looks superficially like the
Common Dolphin but can be distinguished by a dark,
narrow band extending backwards on the flank from the
eye. It has been stranded four times on British coasts.

The Common Dolphin (*Delphinus delphis*) is widely distributed, sometimes in very large schools, in temperate and
warm seas all over the world. It has been known in the
Mediterranean since classical times (The Boy on the Dolphin) and has long held the reputation of saving the lives
of drowning men. The Common Dolphin is difficult to
catch, has an apprehensive temperament and seldom thrives
for long in captivity.

The animal is slender, usually not longer than 2·6 m and
with a narrow but pronounced beak demarcated from the
low forehead by a groove. The dorsal fin leans backwards,
comes to a sharp backwardly directed tip and has a concave
caudal edge. The back is darkly pigmented, the belly white,
and there are light grey or yellow-brown stripes along the
flank. It is a powerful swimmer and probably the swiftest of
all cetaceans. The long jaws bear rows of small conical teeth,
up to fifty in each half-jaw, which are useful for catching
small fishes. From 1913 to 1966, 135 reports of strandings
on the British coasts have been recorded, mostly from the
south and west[28]. It and the Bottlenosed Dolphin are the
most plentiful dolphins in British waters.

3

Baleen Whales

Included in the Mysticeti are the largest living mammals, yet all have lost functioning teeth, and have instead developed whalebone or baleen plates in their huge mouths with which they sieve off an incredible quantity of tiny invertebrates (plankton) as they swim through the sea[11,16]. The evolutionary history of the Mysticeti must have started from some toothed form and indeed it has been suggested that *Patriocetus* could be the connecting link with a basal type (p. 24). It retained functional teeth and yet displayed the beginnings of the telescoping of the skull which is seen in mysticetes. By the Oligocene primitive baleen whales called cetotheres had appeared. These were common by the Miocene and persisted into the Pliocene. They lacked teeth and telescoping of the skull was well advanced but not complete. By the Miocene forms representative of modern Rorquals and Right Whales were in existence.

Mysticetes have a row of up to fifty conical tooth crowns in the jaws of young foetuses; it is probable that these are all absorbed long before birth. In Right Whale foetuses it is possible to see the high arching of the upper jaw bones upon the under surface of which the baleen plates (Fig. 3) will develop. These form a series of parallel flattened plates lined up on each side of the upper jaw at right angles to the long axis of the head. Each horny baleen plate is less than 6 mm thick, in large Right Whales an average single plate is about 3m long and 4–5 cm across. There are some 300–400 plates on each 'side' separated from each other by about 1·2 cm. The plates are shortest at the front and back of each 'side'. In other species the baleen is generally shorter in length but often broader. The outer edge is fairly straight so that, when the mouth closes, the lower lip and gum on the inside of the lower jaw pass upwards close against the outer aspect of a side of baleen plates. The plates are usually bent backwards and inwards as the jaws close so that the flow of water between the plates is controlled. The inner edge of each plate is curved outwards to where the plate ends at its pointed tip. On it is a fringe of frayed out 'hairs' of varying thickness and elasticity which are intertwined to form a sort of strainer. It is this moustache-like arrangement that gives the mysticetes their names, the Greek for moustache being *mystax*—thus mystacial. Water flows into the mouth cavity as the whale swims forwards with its mouth open and passes between the baleen plates leaving the small invertebrates of the plankton caught on the sieve-like fringe. When the mouth closes the tongue helps sweep the masses of plankton towards the throat.

Baleen[10,67] is not all the same colour: it is often black, but may be white, or cream-coloured. The fringe on the inner edge is usually the same colour as the plate, but in a few species it is a different colour. A baleen plate is made of keratin; it is really a greatly developed, keratinized palatal ridge. It consists of two cortical lamellae with a series of tubes arranged in several rows in between. The central tubes of this horny 'sandwich' are the smallest. The tubes extend right through the plate and emerge at its curving inner edge as the hairy fringe. The tubes are not embedded in any connective tissue and they are able to move on each other and thus increase the pliability of each plate. The baleen plates grow continuously throughout the whale's life, steadily replacing what is worn away by the constant wear of sea water and tongue movements. Very young foetuses have no sign of baleen in the mouth, but later, ridges are formed on the palate on which rows of papillae develop. The gum epithelium becomes hypertrophied and then cornified along the edges of the rows of papillae. As the whole complex grows the cornified gum becomes the cortical lamella on each side of the papillae, the tips of which also become cornified to form the baleen tubes. As in the formation of real hairs the central part of

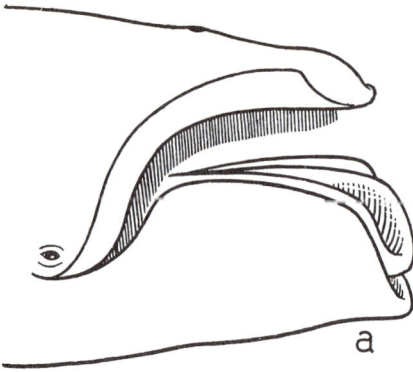

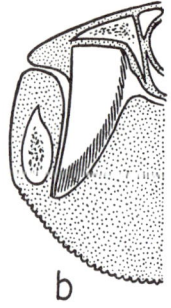

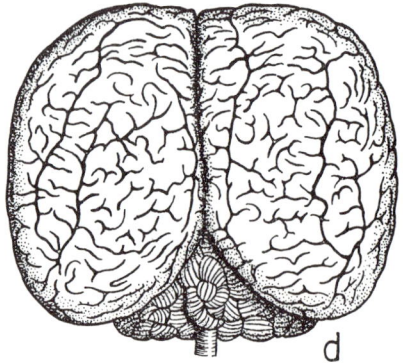

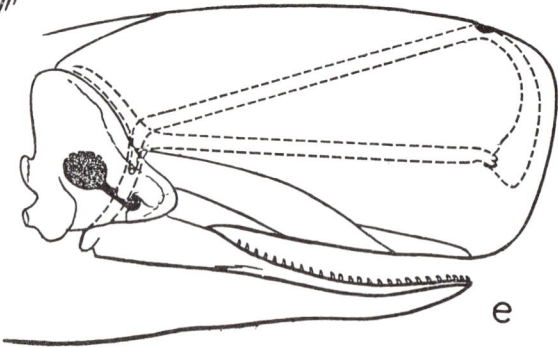

each baleen tube degenerates and leaves a hollow, which in life is fluid filled. The baleen is soft at birth and only hardens after suckling has ceased. The ends of the tubes protruding from the inner aspect of each baleen plate are soon worn away and remain open throughout life. The gum continues to add horny material to the cortical layer of the baleen plate as time passes. The thickest part of the layer will naturally be nearest the base and several attempts have been made to assess the age of a whale by examining the increments of baleen[6][7] laid down (seen as ridges) from the tip to the base of the plate and also the characteristics of the forming baleen within the gum. The process of cornification does not occur at a steady rate and appears to be influenced by metabolic changes resulting from alterations in food supply, general activity and migration, pregnancy and lactation. Rather like the nailbed in a finger the gum and papillae at the base of the forming baleen plate are very vascular. This not only keeps the region warm during exposure to cold sea, but may also, by virtue of changes in blood flow, affect the rate of baleen formation.

The distinction between the cranium and rostrum in the mysticete skull[4] is far less obvious than in odontocetes. In Rorquals the skull forms a gentle curve from front to back, but in Right Whales it is a high arch. In both, the greater proportion of the skull is facial, to carry the baleen. There is no asymmetry. The nostrils are on top of the head, but the direction of the narial cavity is less vertical than in odontocetes, and the nasal bones roof over part of this cavity. The rostrum is again formed by the elongated premaxillae and maxillae, and the ventral surface has a median

---

Fig. 3. Baleen and blowhole. Cetacean brain
- *a* Sketch to show the arrangement of the lips, tongue and a side of baleen in a Rorqual
- *b* The same in cross section
- *c* A plate of baleen with its fringed edge
- *d* Sketch of a cetacean brain from above
- *e* Sketch to show the arrangement of the nasal passages and blowhole in a Sperm Whale

keel, on each side of which is the baleen. Again there is crowding and telescoping of the cranial bones, but it is a distinguishing character of the mysticetes that the maxilla is extended backwards *underneath* the frontal. The supra-occipital forms the entire roof of the cranium, meeting the frontals and excluding, but only just, the parietals from the top of the skull. The orbit is small, but more distinct than in Toothed Whales. It is roofed over by a lateral extension of the frontal, and completed ventrally by the short, relatively thick zygomatic bone. Simple turbinal bones are present. The pterygoids are small and widely separated; they are slightly distended by the air sinuses, which involve them only. The mastoid process is long, but still fits only loosely between the skull bones. The shell-shaped tympanic bulla is easily detached and is frequently brought home by whalers as souvenirs, and because of its resemblance to a human profile, is often decorated to enhance this likeness. The two sides of the lower jaw are rounded in section and laterally bowed. They have only a ligamentous connection at the symphysis. There is a definite coronoid process to the mandible in the Rorquals, but not in the Right Whales. The vast size of the lower jaw and its simple lines have led to it being used, quite frequently, as archways over gates, in churchyards for instance.

In general the mysticete skeleton is similar to that of the odontocetes, but the ribs are more loosely articulated, particularly those of the Pigmy Right Whales where the posterior ten pairs of the very flattened ribs are not articulated at either end. The carpals are formed largely of cartilage, the irregular ossificatory centres increasing in size as the animal grows. The *Right Whales* have the cervical vertebrae fused into a compact mass which presumably gives the anterior part of the axial skeleton distinct strength and rigidity. There is a small pelvic bone and there are remains of a stunted femur and tibia. The flipper is rounded, the five digits being widely spread (except in *Caperea* which has four). The *Rorquals* have the cervical vertebrae unfused, and there are no hind limb remnants. The flipper is long and narrow, achieved partly by the elongation of the radius and ulna, and partly by the elongation and increase in number of the phalanges of the digits, of which there are only four in all forms of Rorqual.

The Order Mysticeti is divided into three families of living whales: the Balaenidae or Right Whales; the Eschrichtidae or Grey Whales (D. F. Eschricht[24] was a Danish cetologist of the mid-nineteenth century) and the Balaenopteridae or Rorquals and Humpback Whale.

FAMILY BALAENIDAE (RIGHT WHALES)

The Right Whales, so-called because at one time they were the 'right' ones to hunt, not only because they were easy to capture but because their baleen and oil made them the 'rightest' prize. They are large, except the Pygmy Right Whale, with enormous mouths, greatly developed lower lips and abundant baleen. They lack grooves beneath the throat and have no dorsal fin, again except in the Pigmy Right Whale. The neck vertebrae are fused into a single unit.

Sadly the Greenland Right Whale (*Balaena mysticetus*) is now so scarce that it is virtually absent in European waters, though numbers are said to be increasing again in Hudson Bay and the Bering Sea. It is a northern form, which never migrates far from the Arctic ice, and was abundant 200 years ago about the coasts of Greenland. The activities of whalers were entirely responsible for its disappearance, made all the more certain by the relative ease of capture of the slow, timid creature. Being slightly lighter than water it was also not so difficult to handle after death.

Full-grown adults are very large, often up to 16 m in total length, sometimes larger still, and the money obtained from the sale of the baleen and oil from one large whale was enough in the eighteenth century to cover the expenses of an expedition. The blubber of the Greenland Right Whale is the thickest of almost all whales. The body has a a large triangular head (thus the name 'Bowhead') up to 6 m in length, and its greatest circumference is just behind the broad paddle-like flippers. It tapers like a cone towards the tail, the last few feet being narrow and cylindrical. The flukes are broad with a central ridge on the dorsal surface. The blowhole consists of two longitudinal slits placed on the highest part of the head well back from its tip. The most striking of all are the two 'sides' of baleen, the central blades of which in the largest whales reached 5 m in length. More than 300 plates are present on each 'side' and with whalebone fetching a maximum of £700 a ton in the eighteenth century it provided a distinct temptation to catch whales of any size. Over a ton of baleen can be obtained from a large animal. The lower lips are very large and well developed, rising high at the sides where they close up against the baleen plates to meet the raised concave arch of the upper lip. Some bristles are present on the front of the jaws. The colour of the whale is predominantly black with areas of white under the chin, and grey on the flippers and near the tail.

What has been written above about the activity of the whale industry leading to the decimation[31, 53] of a species is also true about the Black Right Whales (*Eubalaena glacialis*, etc.). Although often described as separate species, for example the Biscayan Right Whale and forms from the south Atlantic and Pacific, it would seem that there is really only one species which is widely distributed. It was far more abundant centuries ago and was found almost everywhere except in tropical and Arctic waters. Now it is exceptional indeed for more than occasional Black Right Whales to be taken by whalers. They are large whales, in many respects not unlike Greenland Right Whales, but the head is not as large or as long, the upper jaw not so highly arched, the body more evenly curved in outline along the back and there are characteristic excrescences about the mouth, one of which on the front of the upper jaw is known as the 'bonnet'. This protuberance has no known function and is infested with worms and crustaceans (p. 20). The baleen plates are not as long or as numerous as those of the Greenland Right Whale.

Fully grown Pygmy Right Whales (*Caperea marginata*) seldom reach more than 6 m in length. They are confined to southern seas about New Zealand, South America and South Africa and are relatively scarce. They have many of the characteristics of the larger Right Whales, but they do have a small dorsal fin. It is the cetacean with the largest number of ribs: there being only two vertebrae in front of the caudal that lack them. There are only four digits in its small narrow flippers. The baleen plates are small, only about 60 cm in length, but there are 250 of them and the baleen is particularly tough and flexible.

FAMILY ESCHRICHTIDAE (GREY WHALES)

There is but a single genus in this family and it comprises only one form, the Californian Grey Whale[65] (*Eschrichtius robustus*). The generic name used to be *Rhachianectes* which at least was an apt one: when translated, it means 'the swimmer on rocky shores'. There is no doubt that it is a baleen whale, but some of its features it shares with Rorquals, a few with Right Whales. It is seldom over 15 m, the females, as in other baleen whales, being slightly longer. The head is short and the upper jaw arched gently upward, somewhat reminiscent of the Right Whale configuration but nothing like as well developed. There is no distinct dorsal fin, again as in the Right Whale, and there is a succession of low humps, about eight to ten along the dorsal surface of the posterior third of the body. The flukes have a distinct shape, with a concave, rather thick and serrated posterior margin. The flippers are in shape intermediate between those of Right Whales and Rorquals. There are only two to three short grooves beneath the throat, nothing like as many as in Rorquals. This may be associated with the animal being a shallow water form. The baleen is yellowish and the plates are thick, and about 150 in number. The largest plates do not exceed 38 cm in length. The colour of the body is grey, but with much tonal variation and with some lighter markings. There are more hairs on the head region than in any other baleen whale and they are found most plentifully on the tip of the snout. The Californian Grey Whale is found exclusively in the Pacific, though it appears to have existed in the Atlantic in the past. It migrates up and down the Californian coast and along the western Pacific from the Sea of Okhotsk to Korea. When travelling south the whales seem to avoid the coast, but come much closer when returning north. The whale was much hunted in the past by Eskimoes, Indians and American whalers, all taking their toll as the migrating whales passed them.

FAMILY BALAENOPTERIDAE (RORQUALS)

This family includes the Fin Whales or Rorquals[11,38,54], called by these names because they have triangular dorsal fins placed far back towards the tail and also because of the series of parallel grooves or pleats present on the under surface of the throat and chest region (the word Rorqual is said to mean a whale having pleats). Among them are the largest of living animals, the Blue Whales: all except one are world-wide in distribution and all are of commercial importance[31,53]. The head is shorter and flatter than the highly arched one of Right Whales. The flippers are longer and more tapering. The baleen plates are shorter and stiffer, and have particular characteristics in each species. The cervical vertebrae are not fused together. Rorquals also swim faster than Right Whales and are more exciting to hunt. They sink when dead and air has to be pumped into them to keep them afloat. Experts are able to distinguish Rorquals in good weather conditions by the characteristics of the spout or 'blow'.

The Blue Whale[54] or Sibbald's Rorqual (*Balaenoptera musculus*) may reach a length of 30 m when fully grown and weigh up to 10^5 kg. It is a dark slate blue over the whole body, but there may be a diffuse paler mottlings.

The body is more torpedo-like in form than that of a Right Whale and despite its vast size the animal gives the impression of being a fast swimmer. Blue Whales can maintain a speed when submerged of 10–12 knots, reaching 15 knots for short periods. They can dive to well over 500 m and stay submerged for up to 2 hours. The head is about a quarter of the total length and is not relatively as large as that of a Greenland Right Whale. The skull is flattened at the front, almost in a beak-like form, and the lower lips are not raised in the shovel-like manner of Right Whales. Some forty hairs are present on the tip of the lower jaw and a few are present on its sides and on the rostrum. The baleen plates are black and as might be expected from the jaw arrangement are seldom more than 90 cm long, but there are up to 400 plates in each 'side'. There are 60–100 ventral grooves on the under surface of the throat and chest; each is about 5 cm deep and separated by ridges 5–7 cm wide; they extend backwards to behind the point of attachment of the oar-like flippers, almost to the umbilicus. It is thought that the grooves give elasticity to the skin where they are present and so allow distension of the mouth cavity as it fills with water. Their extension farther back along the whale may also help in allowing easier distension of the thorax in deep respiration. The grooves may even be useful during swimming, acting perhaps as a series of shallow 'centre boards' or stabilizers helping to guide the propulsive thrust exerted by the powerful tail and flukes.

Blue Whales seldom congregate in schools, most commonly they are encountered singly or in pairs. They are timid creatures despite their huge size and even banging a bucket or shouting will frighten them. They live almost exclusively on the shrimp-like crustacean *Euphausia superba*, a particular kind of plankton known as krill[11, 29]. It is present in enormous quantities in the cold Antarctic waters, mostly a few fathoms beneath the surface, but more sparsely to considerable depths. The euphausians live on diatoms, particularly *Fragilariopsis antarctica*, which have a definite fat content and are the source of this substance for most

Rorquals. Euphausians also contain carotene, giving the whale's intestine and faeces a characteristically dark red colour. Vitamin A is also present in their eyes and this finds its way to the whale's liver and blubber. The distribution of krill in the ocean depends on several factors, among which the temperature of the water is a primary one. Cold water contains more carbon dioxide, as carbonic acid, and also more oxygen, than warm water. Thus organic matter, vegetable and animal plankton, are up to twenty times as abundant in Antarctic waters as in tropical waters. The distribution is also dependent on the availability of salts and this is governed to a great extent by marine currents of which several important ones are active about the Antarctic pack-ice. Cyclones too affect the krill by causing upheavals of water and bringing younger stages to the surface. Krill is vital in the economy of the life in the regions where it is found; it provides food for fishes, sea-birds, some penguins and seals and also Rorquals. Blue Whales exhibit distinct migratory habits which have been much studied. There is a general movement northwards of southern Blue Whales into warmer waters for breeding during the southern winter. In summer they migrate south-wards for feeding. This results in considerable changes in thickness of the blubber, there being little food for whales in subtropical waters. The metabolic requirements of preg-nancy and lactation also make calls on the blubber as well as it being a source of energy for swimming and keeping up the body-temperature. The Blue Whales of northern waters also migrate, but little is known of their travels in the open seas. It seems that the northern whales prefer to keep to the coasts. In any event it has yet to be shown that members of the northern group intermingle to any extent with those of the southern, though occasional individuals cross the equator, apparently more commonly in the Pacific. This can be explained by the seasonal timing of their ventures north or south. It still seems unlikely, despite their segregation, that they are separate strains. Not all Blue Whales, or any other Rorquals, exhibit this migratory habit, perhaps in relation to reproductive events becoming out of phase with season and feeding habits.

The Common Rorqual or Fin Whale[54] (*B. physalus*) is smaller than the Blue Whale and seldom grows to a length of 24 m. The head is wedge-shaped and the hind part of the back has a marked ridge, from which its name 'Razorback' is derived. The body is light grey above and white below, but there is a characteristic asymmetry of some of the colouring, the lower jaw for instance being white on the right side and pigmented on the left, while the tongue has most colour on the right side. The right side of the baleen is white for a third of its length, while the remainder of that side, and all the left side is grey streaked with yellow, and the fringes of all the plates are white. Fin Whales are encountered in schools, rarely singly, and they can swim remarkably fast. They, too, feed on krill and although often thought to be a distinct type, differentiated in size from the smaller Blue Whale krill, it is the same species of euphausian, the shoals sometimes being composed predominantly of older and thus larger animals. The migratory habits of Fin Whales resemble those of Blue Whales, but do not exactly coincide. Fin Whales return to the Antarctic a little later than Blue Whales. It is possible that air temperature has an effect on the migratory behaviour of the two species.

The Sei Whale (*B. borealis*) is so-called because of its Norwegian name Sejhval, derived from its appearance off certain coasts the same time as the Seje, a species of fish. It reaches a length of some 15–18 m and is rather like the larger Rorquals except for certain features. The head shows a little more arching of the upper jaw; the dorsal fin is large and deeply notched at the back; the body form is a little different and the ventral grooves do not extend tailwards much beyond the level of the tips of the flippers when against the body. The flippers are unusually short. The colour is bluish black to grey with a white area ventrally which varies in extent but never reaches on to the flukes. The baleen plates are characteristically white and the fringe on the inner edge made of such fine hairs that it has an almost woolly quality. The Sei Whale lives on krill and in the north Atlantic on the smaller crustacean *Calanus fin-marchicus* which is effectively trapped in the frilly baleen fringe[39]. It is found in all seas, except very cold ones: it moves towards the poles in the spring, like the Blue Whale, and towards the equator in the autumn, but it keeps well away from the ice floes. But, as with other Rorquals, not all Sei Whales take part in the general migration, particularly those in northern waters. It is of interest that the fastest recorded speed through the water of Rorquals is by a Sei Whale at 35 knots, but it was not maintained for long.

The smallest Rorqual is the Minke Whale or Lesser Rorqual (*B. acutorostrata*) which is 8–9 m long. The head is triangular when seen from above, thus its specific name. The blue-grey whale is often easily distinguished by the white patch on the outer side of the flipper, as if it were wearing a broad bandage, and its white under surface. The baleen too is characteristic, the 300 plates are each less than 30 cm long, often only 20 cm, and are yellowish white in colour. The diet is varied, it includes plankton, herrings, cod and other fish. Minke Whales are usually found in schools of ten to twenty, sometimes up to 100. They are widely distributed but migrate to warmer waters in the autumn and return to colder ones in the spring. They are common on the Norwegian coast, especially in the summer, and get stranded on British coasts (over 100 in 50 years) most often in late summer.

Bryde's Whale (*B. brydei*) is 12–14 m long and more elongated than other Rorquals. It does not differ much from the Sei Whale, but is found only in warm waters off South Africa, in the Bay of Bengal, the Caribbean and the northern Pacific. It does not show any definite migration. The baleen is very characteristic: the white plates, streaked with grey and black in parts, are short (46 cm), broad for their size and with a concave inner margin. The fringe hairs are fairly long and very brittle, little use as a strainer. This Rorqual lives on fish, mainly herring and mackerel, but even quite large sharks and once fifteen apparently unsuspecting penguins. Bryde's Whale has only been distinguished from other Rorquals fairly recently and much has still to be learnt of its habits. If ever any Rorqual were to be kept in captivity for any length of time either this species or the Little Piked Whale are the only reasonable hopes, if only from the practical point of feeding them.

The Humpback Whale[55] (*Megaptera novaeangliae*) is called *Megaptera* because of its very long flippers, reaching almost a third of its length and used to have the specific epithet *nodosa* because of the irregular protuberances on its head and on the lower margin of its flippers. It is probably its rounded appearance on diving that has given rise to the name Humpback. It is a bulky, stout whale reaching to about 16 m in length (Fig. 1). Although not unlike the Rorquals there are sufficient anatomical and behavioural differences to consider it in a separate genus. Besides the features already mentioned the head is short and broad and the dorsal fin is set well back. The tubercles on the head and on the chin and margins of the jaws have one or more short bristles emerging from them, in fact the position of the tubercles corresponds to that of hairs in Rorquals. The pleats beneath the throat and chest are fewer and more widely separated, by ridges up to 20 cm across, than in Rorquals. They extend well back to the umbilicus. The trailing edge of the flukes is scalloped or serrated. The body is black with varying amounts of white underneath and the under surface of the flippers is white. The 400 baleen plates in each 'side' are up to 60 cm in length and are grey to black. Humpbacks eat krill and also small fishes. They are widely distributed in all the great oceans and seem to be more coast loving than Rorquals, though they seldom become stranded and apparently only once on British coasts during the last hundred years. Like Blue and Fin Whales, Humpback Whales exhibit a migratory pattern, and of much the same type. In both southern and northern waters they migrate into warmer waters in the winter. Where possible they pass up along coasts of the great land masses and chains of islands. The timing of their migration does not, however, always coincide with that of Blue and Fin Whales.

The behaviour of Humpback Whales is characteristic. The blow is a short, broad jet. It may perform many very short dives and then sound for periods as long as half an hour. Its way through the water may be slow, erratic and almost casual: it may cruise just below the surface, or even sleep on the surface. It can roll over, its long flipper high in the air, and can even leap quite clear of the water, returning with a spectacular flop. Usually when it dives it does so with a roll, humping its back, and then going vertically down, its flukes remaining momentarily upright above the surface 'like the spread of wings of a great bird'.

4

Some characteristics of Cetacea

All cetaceans are excellent swimmers and divers and their structure is beautifully and impressively adapted for continued existence in water[6,95]. Large whales usually swim rather slowly at between 2 and 5 knots and they can only swim fast for short periods. A maximum speed of 20 knots can only be kept up by a Blue Whale for about 10 minutes. A Californian Grey Whale can cover some 80 nautical miles in a day's swimming of about 20 hours. Whales sleep in the sea on the surface either floating fast asleep with the blowhole above water or swimming very slowly and 'porpoising' lazily. Sperm Whales can sleep so deeply that they are unaware of approaching vessels and have been rammed and killed on more than one occasion. Dolphins do not sleep so deeply and in captivity do not appear to sleep for long periods. It is debatable whether they ever do sleep in the sense that we do, rather they enjoy numerous rests of reduced activity. Dolphins and porpoises can swim so fast and for such long periods that many zoologists have wondered how they obtain the propulsive power to a degree which seems impossible for muscles to provide (Gray's Paradox)[63]. Astonishing speeds have been attributed to them, but the maximum speed of a Common Dolphin does not exceed 20 or 22 knots maintained only for short active bursts. It normally swims at a slower speed of 8 to 12 knots. Bow-riding[26] is a well-known accomplishment of porpoises and dolphins either in front of ships or on surf or wind-generated waves. Some cetaceans use wave-riding as an aid to migratory movements.

It has been suggested that cetaceans can adapt the configuration of their skin to match the contours developed in the water flowing along the flanks. The skin is loose and surprisingly mobile in life, resting on the sponge-like arrangement of the blubber and its connective tissue[25]. Locomotion through the water is thus not accompanied by the production of turbulence waves; there is instead laminar flow along the animal[44]. High-speed underwater photographs have shown that skin waves develop at right angles to the direction of swimming and that the waves are stationary and do not progress in a wave fashion. Frictional drag is reduced by as much as 90 per cent compared with that developed with a rigid surface such as a model of a dolphin would present to the water[42, 45].

Purves[63] has recently shown that the dermal ridges of the corium (Fig. 4) are well developed and that as they may well prevent, as they do in the naked palm of man, sloughing of the epidermis during sheering stresses, their pattern indicates the average flow pattern of water past the animal. He points out that all cetaceans are 'faired' or streamlined all along their dorsal surfaces but only near the tail on the ventral aspect. This suggests that the lower part of the front of the body is propelled through the water at an angle so that it 'breasts' the water rather than driving through it head first. Water would thus flow upwards and backwards relative to the dolphin's body and would thus produce a shearing force, indicated by the lineation of the dermal ridges. The upstroke of the tail is the powerful driving force that propels the dolphin and at the end of the stroke the flukes turn so as to drive water backwards at an accelerated speed. While swimming, the main action of the flippers, again suggested by the dermal ridge pattern, is to lift the front of the dolphin by a hydroplaning effect. Other investigators have suggested that there are special features, physical and chemical, operating at the surface of a dolphin's skin which affect the boundary layer and bring about persistence of laminar flow even at high speeds[6, 45].

The behaviour of cetaceans during swimming—that is to say how long they dive for and how often they surface to blow before or after a long dive and how deep they dive— is very variable[16]. Rorquals can dive for 30–40 minutes but usually only submerge for 5–10 minutes. In between these longer dives they remain on the surface for 5 minutes or longer taking about one breath a minute. If chased or distressed they surface more frequently. During the longer dives they are known to dive often to depths of up to 40 m or deeper and can dive as deep as 500 m. There is really no reason for cetaceans to go to such depths unless being chased or for exploratory gambols as their food is in highest concentration near the surface. Bottlenosed Whales hold the records for length (120 minutes) and Sperm Whales for depth (2,250 m)[20] of dives although the evidence is not altogether convincing. Usually they dive for shorter periods (30–50 minutes) and to nothing like as deep and surfacing for up to 10 minutes taking breaths every 10 seconds or so. Dolphins and porpoises do not dive for as long or as deep. Dives of up to 5 minutes are usual with rapid breaths at the surface at about six breaths a minute. When swimming slowly or idly along resting or asleep they break the water to breathe only three or four times a minute. Dolphins have been trained to dive to over 300 m[95].

SKIN AND BLUBBER

The epidermis of cetaceans is remarkably thin, usually much less than 1 cm thick, with only a few layers of parakeratinized cells in the poorly marked stratum externum[6]. The epidermal cells possess nuclei and are presumably 'alive' much nearer to the surface than in terrestrial mammals. This paucity of protection afforded by the epidermis is seen in the marked scarring that injuries can produce (p. 19) and also in the great sensitivity to sunlight which can raise blisters. The dermis is also thin, thinner even than the epidermis. It contains fat cells only where it merges into the hypodermis or blubber. Numerous dermal papillae (Fig. 4) project up into the epidermis, as many as thirty per square millimetre in some dolphins. They are arranged in definite lines (p. 64) and besides holding the epidermis in place they may allow slight changes in shape of the surface layers. Most of the pigment of dark cetacean skin is found in columnar cells along the sides of the papillae. Blood vessels are present in the papillae and they thus approach close to the skin surface. A network of vessels is also found in the dermis, but the largest vessels traverse the blubber, which is more vascular than usually believed. The usual arrangement is for many thin-walled veins to surround a small artery[6]. Blubber can account for as much as 45 per cent of a whale's body weight and can be up to 60 cm thick. It is only loosely attached to the fascia covering muscles and other parts so that it can be torn away in strips from a large whale at flensing. Blubber varies in thickness[16] over the parts of the body and also it varies with body size, species, seasons, lactation, migration and availability of food supplies. It acts as an insulating blanket encasing the animal and is also an important food store. Blubber is almost lacking or very thin in certain regions, such as round parts of the head and blowhole. It has been calculated that the blubber is usually insufficiently thick and that its heat conducting properties are such that whales are obliged to keep moving continuously otherwise more heat would be lost than is created by metabolic activity. The proportional thickness of blubber[6] in different places on the body is also responsible for the overall shape of a whale and for helping to streamline that shape. When blubber is lost it goes proportionally from all regions so that the configuration of the whale does not alter disadvantageously. Blubber appears to vary in its composition in different regions: the highest fat content is found on the dorsal aspect. The blubber of odontocetes is more waxy in nature than that of the mysticetes. The oil from blubber is used for making soap, margarine and in the paint and leather industries. The component acids of northern and southern whale oils have characteristic differences. The northern varieties are more unsaturated and contain more C_{20} and C_{22} acids and thus resemble marine fish oils. Sperm Whale oil differs in that it consists largely of esters of higher fatty alcohols with higher fatty acids in addition to a certain proportion of triglycerides. For further details the reader should consult T. P. Hilditch *The Chemical Constitution of Natural Fats,* London, 1956.

RESPIRATORY SYSTEM

It is still something of a problem to explain how cetaceans manage to remain underwater for so long on what oxygen is available to them during a dive—apparently only that in the two lungs full of air. The explanation is more complicated than appears on first sight[13, 48]. The volume of air contained in the lungs of a large whale is considerable—estimates show it to be of the order of 2,000 litres—but relative to the size and weight of the whale the lung capacity is not greatly increased. Cetaceans can, however, ventilate the lung more completely than terrestrial mammals, possibly over 90 per cent of the inspired air being changed at each breath. It is likely that the obliquely placed muscular diaphragm (devoid of a central tendon) helps to empty the lung and that an increased range of thoracic movements also assists. Whales also appear to be able to fill their lungs to capacity more easily than land mammals, although there is also much variation at different times in each species depending on whether they are diving or have dived deep and for long periods. The degree to which distension of the thoracic retia (see p. 71) helps to empty the lungs under any particular circumstances, or if at all, is just not known although many authorities maintain that the retia when engorged can occupy space in the thorax[6].

The cetacean trachea is usually short though relatively wide, its shortness associated with the much diminished neck. It is reinforced with cartilages as in other mammals but they are often incomplete and are frequently fused. The lungs are elongated and largest near the apex. They lack any superficial lobulation and are usually not symmetrical because of the presence of an eparterial bronchus on the right side arising at or above the point of division of the trachea into the main stem bronchi. The cartilages of the bronchial tree extend almost to its periphery and always as far as the entrance to the air sacs[12,13,77]. They make the tubes of the bronchial tree particularly rigid and aid in rapid and effective ventilation of the lung during respiration and also resist changes in pressure. The bronchi possess relatively few mucous glands, unlike those of seals in which glands are plentiful. Their walls also contain much elastic tissue which is also widely distributed in other parts of the lung and beneath the pleura. Throughout the bronchial tree of all dolphins, except in the main tubes, there is a succession of myo-elastic valves that break up the bronchi into a series of compartments when the valves are tightly closed (Fig. 4). They are not found in the large cetaceans in which instead there is a strong smooth muscle sphincter about the alveolar ducts. The functions of these valves and sphincters is not clearly understood. It is unlikely that they keep air in the alveoli during dives, but that they allow air to be forced from the alveoli into the bronchial tree and there sequestrate it in the intervalvular compartments where gases are not so intimately related to blood vessels and thus a solution of nitrogen is less likely to occur. Again it may be that the valves regulate the escape of air along the tree and could be involved in the production of the noises dolphins are known to make (p. 79). There appear to be some interesting differences in small and large cetaceans in that the septa separating the alveoli vary in thickness and in content of elastic tissue and smooth muscle, it being most in the largest whales. There are also features of the pulmonary and bronchial vessels, such as their coiled arrangement and the presence of endothelial cushions projecting from the walls in a valvular fashion, all of which may be adaptations to deal with sudden changes in pressure in the lungs and thorax[6,12,13].

The cetacean larynx is an elongated structure that is held protruded into the back of the nasal air passage (p. 15). Vocal cords are absent and although the laryngeal airway seems remarkably narrow and elongated it can be dilated by muscular action. As in other mammals, however, the laryngeal opening appears to be one of the parts of the respiratory system that restricts air flow most; in cetaceans the nasal passage is also narrow and can be completely occluded at the blowhole. These anatomical arrangements all help to procure the forceful almost explosive nature of expiration at the 'blow' (p. 17). The anatomy of the nasal passages is described on p. 15 and that of the blowhole on p. 17. The possible parts played by the air passages in production of sounds is discussed later on p. 80.

It will be realized then that there are no extraordinary features in the respiratory system which particularly aid a cetacean to carry with it markedly increased quantities of oxygen when it submerges. That it carries only its lungs full of air below is obviously in one way to its advantage. Human divers who are continually breathing air during a dive are ventilating the lungs with air that is under pressure. If they return from a depth too rapidly, nitrogen that has become dissolved under pressure in the plasma bubbles out in dangerous places such as in nervous tissue and joints and can cause damage and great pain. This causes the condition known as caisson sickness or the 'bends'. Whales submerge after taking only one breath. When the air is compressed it is forced into 'safe' regions of the respiratory pathway. It is maintained that the air sinuses at the base of the skull that are derived from the pharyngo-tympanic tube and tympanic cavity (p. 82) play an important part in absorbing nitrogen in the oily material which they contain. The 'spout' is said to contain a fine emulsion of this material in the form of a foam[30]. Whales thus avoid caisson disease and can safely come rapidly to the surface from great depths.

There are three important factors which enable whales to remain submerged for so long on such apparently limited oxygen[13]. The first is the possession by their muscles of large quantities of myohaemoglobin, as much as ten times that found in the muscles of terrestrial mammals and with high oxygen-storing properties. The muscles carry, as it were, their own peripheral oxygen stores with them on a dive. Secondly, it appears that marine mammals generally are less sensitive to the effects of accumulating lactic acid and carbon dioxide in their circulation. Their muscles are also able to act anaerobically for longer than in terrestrial mammals. Thirdly, there is growing evidence that there is a redistribution of arterial blood during a dive and that through peripheral vasoconstriction oxygenated blood is mainly reserved for essential organs such as the brain. Changes in heart rate occur in seals during a dive (p. 135): what adjustments are thought to occur in the vascular system of cetaceans are discussed in the next section. It is also thought, but has yet to be proved, that there may be alterations in certain metabolic processes in various tissues and organs thus conserving utilization of oxygen. Whales are able to dive for so long, therefore, by using peripheral oxygen stores, by anaerobic metabolism, by a redistribution of blood, by being relatively insensitive to chemical stimuli that would increase respiratory activity and possibly by changes in metabolic activity, at least in certain organs and tissues.

CARDIOVASCULAR SYSTEM

There have been few recordings made of the heart rate of cetaceans; practical difficulties in obtaining electrocardiographic tracings are obvious[6,13]. What is known is that the heart rate of the largest whales at the surface is very slow, varying between eight and twenty-three beats a minute. Observations on captive porpoises and dolphins give a heart rate of about 120, again at the surface of the water. It is difficult to be quite certain, because of the natural apprehensiveness of dolphins, but what experiments have been done do not suggest a profound diving bradycardia as exhibited by seals (p. 135). Slijper[16] has investigated the anatomy of the cetacean heart[66] and from its weight relative to that of the body, its shape and its characteristics, concludes that it is not radically different from that organ in other mammals. In no single feature is it more efficient or more powerful than that of a terrestrial mammal, and in the largest whales there is some indication that the situation is indeed reversed. There is also no evidence that the blood volume is increased relative to the body weight, as it is in seals.

There are, however, a number of interesting modifications in the peripheral vessels, of which the most striking are the massive plexuses, the retia mirabilia[6,13]. These are vascular networks, mainly of arteries but with some thin-walled veins among them, embedded in adipose tissue. They are found to a variable extent on each side of the vertebral column between the ribs and outside the pleura (thoracic retia) and also in many other places. Depending on the species, retial masses may extend into the cervical and lumbar regions and into the chevron canal. They may also be present in the spinal canal, usually surrounding the spinal cord, or part of it, and at the base of the brain. Retial tissue often surrounds the optic nerve and may also be related to certain large arteries[21].

Four main types of retial tissue have been recognized: (a) diffuse plexiform anastomoses of arteries and veins in the limbs; (b) vascular bundles enclosed in sheaths; (c) thoracic retia in which the arteries anastomose among themselves, but which also contain veins—these are the cetacean retia; (d) arterial plexuses not associated with veins—such a plexus is found related to the internal carotid of *Globicephala*. Lastly, the large plexuses of veins that are found under the skin and in relation to the abdominal and pelvic walls must be mentioned. As they are really massive venous plexuses they are not really retia, though some writers include them under this heading.

It must first be emphasized that retia are also found in terrestrial mammals, particularly in sloths and some primates. Retia are not, therefore, necessarily associated solely with a marine existence. There has been much discussion about the function of the retia and various hypotheses have been advanced to account for their presence[6,13]. None is, however, entirely satisfactory. It is unlikely that any of the earlier suggestions provide the answer; retia are not, for instance, associated with slow or sustained muscle movements. They do indeed act to some extent as blood reservoirs: the amount of elastic tissue in the walls of both arteries and veins suggests that they can be considerably dilated. The quantity of blood they could contain, however, has been calculated as being insufficient to be of much use after a dive has progressed for more than a few minutes. Some retia certainly assist venous return, help to maintain steady blood flow either actively or passively, and also act as devices preventing intermittent interruptions of blood flow caused by muscular or other pressure. Retia at the base of the brain may help provide a continuous and steady flow of blood to the brain tissue that is unaffected by any fluctuations in heart rate on diving. Other retia play a part in conserving heat, transferring heat from arteries passing to fins, flippers or flukes to the surrounding thin-walled veins[68]. The cooling effect of cold sea water on blood circulating through the whale's appendages is thus reduced (counter-current vascular heat exchange).

It seems likely that the main retial masses of cetaceans are concerned with alleviation of pressure changes that develop during diving[61,75]. There is virtually no experimental evidence to support this contention but little to back any other. It can be argued, and there is increasing evidence to support such a necessity, that the air pressure within the respiratory tract is not continuously the same as that experienced by the rest of the whale's body during a dive. Active movements of the thorax or diaphragm may occur underwater to produce the sounds needed for echo-location (p. 79). Pressure differences between those in the thorax, abdomen and vascular system must be corrected to within physiological limits and many authors have suggested that the retia engorge with blood and act as 'space-fillers' in the thorax during a dive. The numerous anastomoses within and between retial masses enable a balanced and equitable distribution of blood in various parts of the body, also perhaps preventing overloading or engorgement of particularly sensitive or delicate regions such as the brain and spinal cord.

Relative to the size of the animals the veins are not as enlarged as those of pinnipeds, though the posterior vena cava is dilated in the hepatic region in some species. The posterior vena cava shows marked variation in its anatomy not only in different species but even within a species[6,92]. It is not uncommon to find the vessel duplicated as far cranial as the level of the renal arteries. There is, however, marked difference in the arrangement of its tributaries relative to the aorta: it is also not uncommon to encounter a single posterior vena cava formed by the union of several large tributaries in the pelvis. There are always plentiful anastomoses between the caval venous system and the extra-dural veins within the spinal canal. Two, often very large, veins are present *ventral* to the spinal cord, though as in *Phocoena* there may be only one. They are usually surrounded by retial tissue for some part of their course, particularly at the more cranial end of the vertebral column. The significance of these vessels and their communications is discussed on p. 131.

Some dilatation of the hepatic veins is found within the liver substance in some odontocetes, but it is rare or hardly marked in mysticetes. There is no real caval sphincter (p. 133) in cetaceans, though in odontocetes the diaphragm is continued about the posterior vena cava in the form of a sling or as slips of muscle that could have some sphincteric action on the vena cava. No evidence of a true hepatic sinus has yet been seen in cetaceans. The main renal vein leaves the cetacean kidney at its hilum from the mesial slit. There is also a superficial subcapsular plexus, but it is not as marked as in pinnipeds (p. 133) and may be absent as in *Caperea*. The azygos system, well developed in seals, is either absent altogether in cetaceans or is much reduced to a slender vessel on the right side. It has been suggested that in the species where it is found the large vein leaving the first right thoracic intervertebral foramen to join the anterior vena cava does represent the arch of the azygos vein[92]. John Hunter maintained that the lack of the azygos system in whales was associated with the presence of large

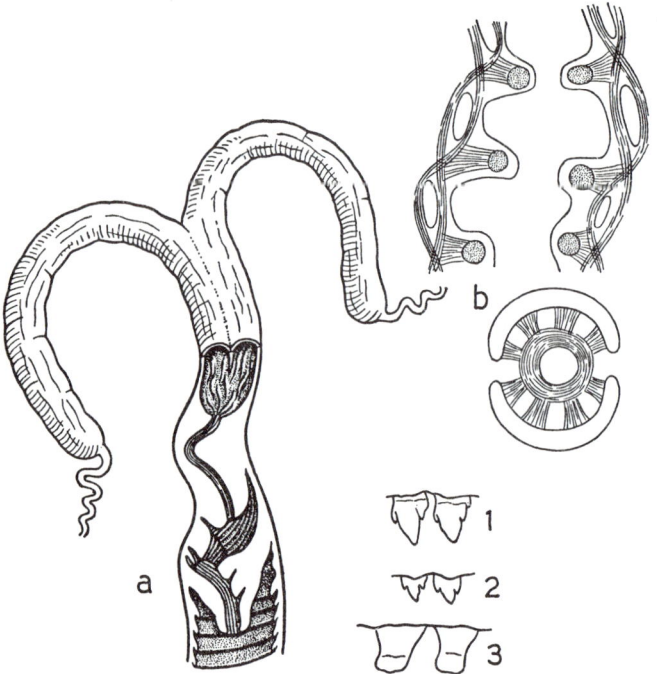

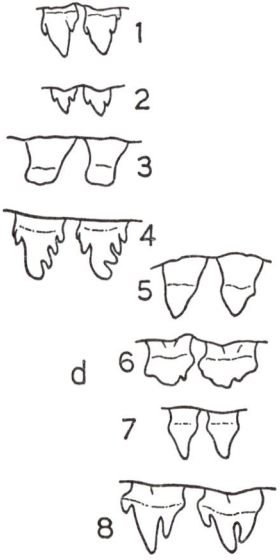

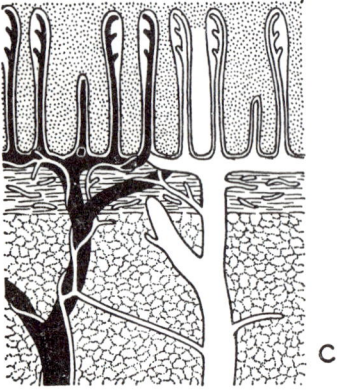

spinal veins taking over its functions, but in view of the
large azygos in pinnipeds it seems more likely that it is
replaced by the retial masses.

ALIMENTARY CANAL

The cetacean stomach[33] consists of three main compartments, a fore-stomach devoid of glands and lined by
squamous epithelium, a main stomach with a folded mucosa
and gastric glands, and a relatively smooth pyloric stomach
which may be bent on itself or show several dilatations and
which has some glands in its walls. The cetacean fore-
stomach is homologous[16] with the proventriculi (rumen,
reticulum and omasum) of cattle and can be considered as
an oesophageal sacculation. If often contains stones and
pebbles of varying size which with the powerful contractions
of the muscular walls help to grind up fish bones or crus-
tacea. The fore-stomach is larger in odontocetes: Beaked
Whales which feed on cuttle-fish lack one. The main cetacean
stomach is equivalent to the fundic portion of a simple
mammalian stomach or to the abomasum of cattle. Its
glands produce a gastric juice containing pepsin, hydro-
chloric acid and some lipase. The pepsin was isolated for
pharmaceutical purposes in Japan. The proventricular and
main compartments of the stomach of large whales can
hold 1,000 kg of krill (p. 57). The pyloric compartment is

Fig. 4. Cetacean viscera. Seal teeth

    a Drawing of the vagina, vaginal folds and uterus of a Pilot
       Whale

    b Sketch of the intrabronchiolar myo-elastic valves in the
       lungs of odontocetes, left in longitudinal section, right in
       transverse. After Slijper[16]

    c Diagram of the blood supply of the surface of the blubber
       and dermal papillae of a porpoise. After Parry

    d Outline of cheek teeth of 1. Australian Fur Seal; 2. Ringed
       Seal; 3. Southern Elephant Seal; 4. Crabeater; 5. Southern
       Sea Lion; 6. West Indian Monk Seal; 7. Grey Seal;
       8. Leopard Seal

equivalent to the pyloric region of the abomasum of cattle. It leads by a narrow pylorus into the duodenum, the first part of which is sometimes markedly dilated.

The intestine is remarkable for its length, it is probably longest in Sperm Whales. There is no clearly defined caecum and so it is difficult to tell where the small intestine continues into the large. The detailed histology of the delphinid intestine[6] has been described but not whether there is much difference in fish or krill eaters. The food taken by cetaceans is discussed in Chapters 2 and 3. The characteristics of ambergris, the curious material produced in the intestine of Sperm Whales are described on p. 36. The main difficulty confronting anyone wishing to investigate the histological features of the alimentary canal of cetaceans is that the length of time elapsing between death and removal of tissue is so long that reasonable fixation is virtually impossible. For the same reason little is known about the pancreas and most of the other endocrine[2] and exocrine organs.

The liver is usually bilobed but a third lobe is sometimes present. It can weigh 1,000 kg in the largest whales and whale-liver oil is extracted for its high vitamin A content. There is no gall bladder.

The thyroid gland[72] is large relative to the body weight, as has been found in other marine mammals[2]. This has been related to the need for a high metabolic rate in animals which are liable to lose much heat if they are not continuously active. What is known of the adrenal glands suggests that they are relatively small compared to the body weight. The pituitary has a large anterior lobe[2,12] that is distinctly separated from the posterior lobe by an intervening septum.

EXCRETORY ORGANS

The cetacean kidney is divided into numerous lobules or renules (Fig. 5). Up to 3,000 may be counted in a kidney of the largest whales whereas a dolphin has 300–650[12]. Each renule is a distinct entity with its own blood supply, pyramid and calyx and a collecting duct leading from it to join neighbouring ones and pass to the ureter. Sometimes adjoining renules are fused together. There is only a poorly developed superficial renal plexus[92] of veins such as is present in phocids (p. 133) and it may be absent altogether, the venous drainage being through one or two main renal veins leaving the kidney at its mesial slit together with the ureter. When the superficial plexus is present it usually drains into the renal vein though it has been denied that there is any anastomosis or communication between these internal and external venous pathways and the suggestion has been made that the superficial plexus is acting as a form of portal circulation from the renules back to the vena cava.

The significance of the lobulation is not clear. It has been shown that cetaceans, like seals, produce large quantities of urine after a meal[13,27]. The source of the water is said to be from the oxidation of fats and of course from food taken in. Every five kilogrammes of fish eaten could give rise to nearly four litres of water. It is maintained that cetaceans do not deliberately drink sea water, though some cannot help but be taken in with krill and fish. The lobulation of the kidney could provide an increased number of glomeruli to cope with the production of the greater amount of urine. The fresh-water dolphin *Platanista* has a smaller number of renules (80) than that (250) of a sea-water porpoise half its size. Slijper[16] argues that this indicates a relation between lobulation, increase of renal cortical tissue and a marine existence. He also points out that large Rorquals have a high kidney to body weight ratio. The ratio is in fact higher in all cetaceans in which it has been measured than in terrestrial mammals and man. It is highest in Bottlenosed Dolphins (1·1 per cent) and several species of porpoise.

It is also possible that lobulation of the kidney could indicate that presence of independent renal units in a physiological sense as well as anatomical. Although still only speculative it might be that through some intrinsic neuro-vascular mechanism only a few renules, or groups of them, act at any one time unless there be excessive demands on renal function when the whole organ becomes active. It is still a little puzzling, however, that such marked lobulation does occur for, as has occasionally been pointed out, the glomerular filtration rate that is normally found in mammalian kidneys should be adequate to deal with cetacean clearance problems even if they demand the production of much urine. Recently it has been suggested that the renicular arrangement is involved in efficient discharge of urine from the medullary papillae. A perimedullary muscular basket or sporta[12,19] has been described in several cetacean species. The muscular activity of the sporta appears sufficient to have a compressing or milking action on the excretory ducts (of Bellini) and so assist the discharge of urine into the calyx. This implies a positive expression of urine out of the terminal ducts and if it is an essential requisite in cetacean excretion it would clearly be more efficient if it took place in renules rather than in a whole organ. Insufficient investigations have been made on other cetaceans species to know whether this muscular sporta is related to deep diving. Not unnaturally almost nothing is known about renal functions in cetaceans though there is some interesting evidence that dolphins can for short periods excrete urine with a salt concentration higher than found in terrestrial mammals especially after a meal.

Little is known about the capacity of the bladder or the composition of urine. The bladder is usually described as being relatively small: there is obviously little point in there being a large storage viscus in an animal that can micturate so readily without soiling its environment. The narrowing of the cetacean pelvic region to form the tail may also be associated with the relatively small bladder. The few investigations of the urine that have been made suggest that it has normal mammalian composition and constituents[13,27]. The urethra, penis and urogenital openings are described on p. 18.

HEARING AND SOUND PRODUCTION

Hearing is the most important of the special senses for all cetaceans[30]. As the sense of smell is either totally lacking or else much reduced and as the turbidity of the water restricts even the most acute vision, cetaceans rely on their sense of hearing to tell them where they are under water. How they do it has only recently become apparent[12,22,42]. Although hydrophonic detection of noises made by dolphins occurred frequently during the Second World War it was not realized for what reason the noises were made.

Dolphins emit two kinds of sound; one is a shrill whistle which varies between 7,000 and 15,000 cycles per second with a continuously changing pitch. Other odontocetes emit a whistle of lower pitch, even as low as 500 cycles per second. It seems certain that dolphins use these sounds to make contact with each other when swimming in herds. The whistling noises are sometimes loud enough to be heard by a man standing above the water. Those made by White Whales are almost like shrill screams and have given rise to the nickname of 'Sea Canary' for this form. Various other whistling sounds have been recorded as being made by cetaceans: whining, squeaking and mooing, as well as bellowing, grunting and growling are terms that have been used to describe these noises. Low pitched humming and whistling is produced by Rorquals and the long, continuous, very complicated and repeated 'song' of the Humpback Whale is now well known.

The second type of sound produced by dolphins resembles that made by a creaking gate or door. They are supersonic sounds emitted as a series of short pulses of variable duration with a frequency between 20,000 and 200,000 cycles per second (the human ear can detect sounds up to a frequency of 25,000 cycles). The animals apparently use these pulses to echo-locate objects or food under water. They 'learn' their way about new surroundings and 'position' new objects or obstacles placed in the water. When blindfolded they can still swim around tanks and detect fish, behaving as if they could in fact see them. They seem only to be defeated by gradual slopes, very thin wires, nets of very coarse mesh and sometimes by suddenly encountering square corners. This echo-location by use of sonar signals enables them to detect most nets, barriers and other obstacles beneath the water and if necessary they can jump out of water to clear them. Much research is centred on how dolphins can produce these supersonic pulses but the problem has not been finally solved. Cetaceans have no vocal cords though a noise can be produced by blowing air through the larynx. It is not impossible that the diverticula in relation to the blowhole act as resonators, or even that their valves or plugs can be made to vibrate. The numerous myo-elastic valves in the bronchial tree (p. 68) play some part in regulating the passage of air into the rest of the respiratory tract. It is possible for us to make intermittent squeaking noises with the mouth shut and the nostrils held in the fingers while at the same time passing air forcefully forwards and backwards from the lungs to the nasopharynx. Perhaps dolphins have perfected such a mechanism to produce their supersonic noises, though it is still not known how much, or if at all, the blowhole itself takes part in producing or modulating the noises. Air is certainly released from the blowhole during a dive but this does not mean that sound is being emitted at the same time and there may be quite another explanation for its escape. It is, however, difficult to imagine where the noises are made if not produced in the respiratory tract.

That all cetaceans have an acute sense of hearing has been known since Aristotle, though he denied that there was an external meatus. It used to be thought that hearing in cetaceans underwater was by bone conduction. Others[30] have maintained, however, that hearing in whales is carried out by way of the external auditory meatus, tympanic membrane and auditory ossicles just as in terrestrial mammals. Hearing is acute and a wide range of frequencies can be detected: it is also discriminative and directional.

The external auditory meatus in the Delphinidae is patent from near the external pit to the tympanum[30]. It is kinked as it traverses the subcutaneous tissues and its lining is usually pigmented. The curvature is maintained by a dorsally placed muscle passing to the skull. Ear cartilages are related to the meatus and vestigial outer ear muscles have been described. In Rorquals and Humpbacks the meatus is straighter, but is closed for part of its length and is there represented by a solid cord which may have small cavities in it. The inner, medial, part of the meatus contains the ear-plug[64] mentioned on p. 92. The cetacean tympanic membrane consists of two parts, a fibrous portion with an external concavity and a non-fibrous portion which projects into the external auditory meatus. In the Balaenopteridae the non-fibrous portion is so greatly enlarged that it resembles a glove finger pushing outwards into the meatus. The rounded base of the ear-plug fits onto the outer end of this glove-finger extension: both the glove-finger and the ear-plug can be moved actively by muscular contraction. It has been found that the ear-plug is an excellent conductor of sounds of a very high pitch, particularly in a longitudinal direction.

There are several other interesting features about the auditory mechanism in cetaceans, and they have only recently been clearly explained[30]. The tympanic membrane is attached to an annular opening in the petro-tympanic bone and from it vibrations are conveyed along the band-shaped tympanic ligament to the handle of the malleus. In all cetaceans the tympanic is a shell-shaped bone—the tympanic bulla—which is attached to the skull by two thin processes (only one in odontocetes) and by its shape enlarges the middle ear cavity. As the strangely shaped bone is easily broken off it is frequently kept as a souvenir of whaling days. Both the petrosal and tympanic bones are almost completely isolated from the skull (at least by osseous connection) by a well-developed pterygoid air sinus that is really an extension of the tympanic cavity. This dissociation of the periotic bony complex from the skull bones and the degree of development of the air sinuses is not equivalent in all cetaceans. It is seen least developed in *Caperea* and most in the Delphinoidea. Also helping to isolate the ear bones is a variably developed peribullary air sinus and a closely adherent fibro-elastic capsule about the outside of the bulla which is as much as 10 cm thick in a large whale. The sinuses and tympanic cavity are filled with a foamed, oil-mucus emulsion the liquid components of which are produced by glands in the lining of the sinus. There is evidence that nitrogen becomes dissolved in the foam in the air sacs and that some foam is discharged at expiration. The air sacs are mainly limited to the ear region in mysticetes but are spread more extensively over the base of the skull in odontocetes. They are surrounded by a venous plexus that lies between two tough layers of fibrous tissue which are the de-ossified remnants of the pterygoid laminae.

The air sacs system about the ear, and probably also the fibro-venous plexus, play two important roles in hearing by cetaceans, which it must be recalled dive to considerable depths and if they are to use the tympanic membrane will have to achieve equilibrium in pressure on its inner and outer aspects. Terrestrial mammals accomplish this equilibrium easily by way of the pharyngotympanic tube and naso-pharynx but cetaceans are denied this route except on sur-facing. During a dive of fluctuating depth there could be considerable changes in pressure of the air in the tympanic cavity. Fraser and Purves[30] consider that 'at all times during swimming and diving an equilibrium is maintained between (a) the hydrostatic pressure, (b) the rigidity of the tissues, (c) the turgor pressure of the blood vascular system, (d) the viscosity of the foam and (e) the volume of the gas as determined by the gas laws and by solution of the contained gas in the oil and mucus'. Their paper should be consulted for more details of the importance of the air sacs, particularly in respect of their second function, that of procuring acoustical isolation of the periotic. It would seem fairly certain that it is the foam in the sacs that is the principal factor bringing about this isolation and ensuring that sounds are transmitted through the ear drum and not by conduction through the bone, blubber or other tissues of the body.

The tympanic bulla is made of very hard, dense bone, much heavier than that of the rest of the skeleton. It is possible that this also helps isolate the periotic complex in that the heavier bone will not resonate at low frequencies transmitted by the lighter tissues. The ear ossicles are stout and heavy and the malleus is attached to the tympanic bulla by a bony connection. The fusion is obtained in a manner such that vibrations of the tympanic bulla are not transmitted to the incus, whereas those passing along the tympanic ligament are. The malleo-incudal joint is deep and striking and the stapes, although less obviously stirrup-shaped and often lacking an intercrural foramen, fits snugly into the fenestra ovalis but it is not ankylosed there. There is in the cetacean middle ear a mechanism for the increase of displacement amplitude of water-borne sounds and the method of amplification is self-compensating. All the evidence suggests that the cetacean auditory apparatus is put into action by transmission of sounds through the tympanic membrane and that it is ingeniously adapted for the reception of sounds of a very high frequency and with marked discrimination. What investigation there has been of the cochlea suggests that the receptor cells of the organ of Corti near the fenestra ovalis are large and well developed—again suggesting an adaptation in favour of reception of high frequency sounds.

Directionality in hearing is obtained in terrestrial mammals as a result of the anatomical separation of the two ears and the screening effect of the head allowing assessment of differences of phase and intensity of sounds. The presence of an external pinna and ability to move the head on a neck enhance the direction sense. Cetaceans lack a pinna, have a stunted neck and a remarkably small opening to the external meatus. Fraser and Purves[30] produce evidence that indicates that directionality can be obtained in cetaceans by altering the tension in the meatal tube with the auricular muscles. They also suggest that the pterygoid and palatal muscles, which have insertions on the walls of the air sacs, can exert a powerful influence on pressure in the tympanic cavity, thus affecting the tension of the tympanic membrane to a degree greater than that produced by the tensor tympani. Such a mechanism could enhance directional hearing at the great depths cetaceans are known to be able to reach.

THE NERVOUS SYSTEM

A considerable literature on the cetacean brain[18,35] and nervous system has accumulated since the days of John Hunter's classic work on the anatomy of whales. With the recent discovery of the sometimes astounding ability of dolphins to learn and the possibility that they can communicate, investigations of their brain have received a great stimulus. It has been known since antiquity that dolphins love to play and that they have a friendly disposition towards each other and even members of other species of cetacean and man. Much more has been discovered about their abilities since they have been kept in captivity.

The brain of the largest cetaceans[12] is heavier than that of any other mammal: the record weight is that for the brain of a Sperm Whale[43] at nearly 8 kg or about 0·03 per cent of the body weight. (A human brain weighs about 1,400 g or 1·93 per cent of the body weight: of other mammals only an elephant has a brain heavier at about 4·5 kg.) A Bottlenosed Dolphin's brain weighs over 1,400 g, about 1·2 per cent of the body weight, and that of a porpoise just over 400 g and over 0·85 per cent of the body weight. The weight of a brain is not of course in itself an indication of any particular degree of intelligence, it increases in size mainly in relation to an increase in the surface area of a mammal. Those animals of equal body weight, though of different orders, which show increased brain weight and usually higher organization of cerebral centres are said to be more highly 'cephalized'. Various coefficients of cephalization have been devised and for what they are worth show that odontocetes have the most developed brains, some not far below that of man. It does not necessarily follow, however, that mysticetes are that much less intelligent. Their body weight is nearly 30 per cent blubber and this figure fluctuates markedly with seasonal and other variations. It is now realized that the ratio of various parts of the brain to each other and to the total brain weight can provide better clues to brain functional ability than the ratio of brain to body weight.

The cetacean brain and its cerebral hemispheres in particular appear much foreshortened and widened transversely[12,18]. There is a little evidence, though it is not generally accepted, that this shortening and brachencephaly might have occurred before and independently of the telescoping of the skull. Breathnach[18] writes: 'The relation between the skull and brain should rather be seen as one of mutual adaptation occurring over a long period, in which any direct stress on the brain was minimal'. The possible effect of intracranial tissues such as retial masses on brain shape is impossible to assess. Some authors have described an asymmetry in brain shape, especially in odontocetes, which have an asymmetrical skull, but the large size of the brain in mysticetes makes proper fixation difficult.

The cetacean brain is characterized by a striking development of the telencephalon with marked convolution of the cerebral cortex[6,18,46,47]. The degree of complexity of the convolutions and their depth approach that of man (Fig. 3). The sulcal pattern, however, bears more resemblance to that of carnivores and ungulates. What investigation of the cellular features has been done suggests that although five or more layers can be discerned in the cerebral cortex[12] (isocortex) of some cetaceans, neurone density is low and the basic cytoarchitectonic structure is said to be different from that in other mammals. These findings are not necessarily associated with a low mental capacity, for in mammals generally cortical neurone density decreases with increasing brain weight. The allocortex, the unlayered more primitive cortex, has been shown to display a degree of differentiation much greater than previously realized. It has been maintained that the great development of the cetacean forebrain is associated with marked muscle development and the need for the more highly organized nervous system that skilful swimming would demand. As will be shown certain parts of the brain are indeed developed in this connection but it seems unlikely that an animal that uses its tail primarily for propulsion (p. 64) would have so large a brain if other faculties were not involved.

Other parts of the cetacean central nervous system are also interestingly developed, in particular the cerebellum on which much original work has been done by Jansen[36,37]. He made great use of embryological material and has shown that although the structure of the cerebellum conforms to the general mammalian pattern there are certain characteristic features. These include an enlargement of paraflocculus, probably associated with afferents arising in the cerebral hemispheres and upper brain stem, and a large lobulus simplex and paramedian lobule. Jansen decided that the lobulus simplex received tactile sensation from the head region and that the paraflocculus was associated with the trunk, tail and fluke sensory input. Other parts of the cerebellum, such as the anterior hemispheres, the ansiform lobule and flocculo-nodular lobe are reduced in size. This has been associated with the relative lack of demand for equilibration in a medium such as water in which a whale floats naturally the right way up as opposed to the much more complex situation facing a terrestrial mammal. There is little relative development of the vestibular apparatus and the flocculo-nodular lobe, which receives vestibular afferents, is reduced in size as stated above. Vestibular activity is therefore not a factor increasing cerebellar size. We know, however, that even if as is nowadays thought, cetaceans do not need an increased sense of equilibrium, they do display remarkable powers of muscular co-ordination. On any reckoning it needs considerable skill to swim underwater 20 m or so across a tank and then jump 7 m clear of the water to take a cigarette from an attendant's mouth. It has not unnaturally been suggested that the cerebellum, the basal ganglia, the red nucleus and various other parts of the nervous system are implicated in obtaining such precision swimming. They almost certainly are, but as Breathnach[18] continues: 'the precise manner in which they work is unknown . . . these functions depend on the integrated activity of many parts of the nervous system. Accordingly, any attempt to associate specializations in the muscular arrangement, or activity of cetaceans with particular features of the brain, is liable to frustration from the outset'.

The importance of auditory mechanisms[23,30] in cetaceans has already been emphasized and not surprisingly the cochlear nucleus in the brain stem, the trapezoid body, the lateral lemniscus and the inferior colliculi are all enlarged, more in the odontocetes perhaps than in mysticetes. All this reinforces the importance of the auditory pathways. Unfortunately little is known about the auditory projections to the cortex, though Langworthy[46] considers that a large area of the cortex must be involved and that the large size of the temporal lobe supports his view.

Langworthy[46] attributes only a subsidiary role to visual, trigeminal and general sensory impressions in the differentiation of the cetacean cortex. There has been some controversy as to the degree of visual acuity cetaceans possess and whether they can see as well in air as in water. Some have maintained that sight in air is poor because of myopic vision in this medium and that even in water perception is limited to small moving objects or large stationary ones. It is said that the structure of the retina shows sparsely distributed ganglion cells each fed from many rods, so reducing discrimination, and that cones are absent. Some cetaceans, however, may be amphiophthalmic in that images of objects in different media pass to different segments of the retina with axes of unequal length or different orientation. Recent observations on dolphins[42] suggest that their sight in air is as good as that of most mammals. The optic nerve is relatively small, though larger in odontocetes; in the Gangetic Dolphin it is thread-like in thinness. The lateral geniculate body, the structure of which can be a guide to the degree of visual acuity, is large in *Tursiops* but does not exhibit any lamination. In other cetaceans it is small and circumscribed but much more investigation will have to be done of both this body and the superior colliculus, which always appears quite distinct in cetaceans, but about which more must be learnt. Little again is known of the visual cortex: it has been said to be absent and also to be developed as well as that in other mammals. The authors have no doubt at all that Bottlenosed Dolphins can see quite well out of water and that they take great interest in their surroundings.

The trigeminal is the largest cranial nerve in mysticetes and it seems likely that the oral region is highly sensitive[19]. The hairs, bristles and tubercles found in the snout region of some cetaceans may be tactile structures. The generally held view that cetaceans have their cutaneous and proprioceptive sensibilities poorly developed has been challenged recently. It has even been claimed that they are insensible to pain, but many investigations[6,13] have shown that in certain regions at least some odontocetes have an abundant and interesting cutaneous innervation. All odontocetes possess an adipose cushion, more or less well developed, in the snout region above the upper jaw. It is often called the 'melon' and is profusely supplied by branches of the trigeminal nerve. The function of this region is not really understood but it has been suggested that there are tactile endings in the cushion which respond to increases in water pressure and may even register water flow. Mysticetes also have sensory receptors in the head region.

Olfactory nerves and bulbs are lacking in all odontocetes[18,23]: they have been demonstrated in foetal mysticetes, but there is some doubt whether they are present in adults. Edinger[23] considers that they are present but are missed when the brain is removed. The absence or marked reduction of the olfactory nerves, bulbs and secondary connexions is almost certainly not related to the shape of the cetacean brain, nor have they necessarily become reduced as a result of the auditory centres becoming the dominant special sense. Investigation of the tertiary olfactory centres within the cetacean brain has led to varying and ambiguous conclusions, made worse by the fact that we do not really yet understand the real significance of what is found in the various parts of the brain alleged to be concerned with a sense of smell. The condition of the cetacean hippocampus is an excellent example of the difficulties encountered. Its characteristics could be used to support either an olfactory or a non-olfactory thesis as to its function. It is generally concluded, however, that cetaceans have no or little sense of smell in water: indeed the sea is said not to have any contact with the regions innervated by olfactory fibres. Unfortunately, studies of the cetacean rhinencephalon, in its widest sense, have helped little towards localizing olfactory functions in the brain. Studies on the brain stem and cord[18,37] have suggested the alleged lack of skin sensibility because of the smallness of the number of fibres in the dorsal roots of spinal nerves, the relatively small size of the posterior horns and the sensory fibre tracts and the poor development of the nucleus gracilis and cuneatus. Virtually no experimental work has been performed to test the validity of these suggestions. There seems little doubt that part at least of the skin is sensitive to air as the stimulus to a dolphin to breathe is the feeling of air on the skin about the blowhole when it breaks the surface. It is also the impression of many who have studied dolphins in captivity that their skin is much more sensitive than has hitherto been believed though possibly not to temperature changes. There is known to be a rich cutaneous sensory innervation in the region of the urogenital opening in both sexes and the penis is often used as a tactile organ. Dolphins in captivity enjoy playing with air bubbles and appear to gain pleasure with their contact on certain areas of skin.

The spinal cord also shows certain features associated with the modification of the fore-limb as a flipper, the absence of hind limbs, the absence of hair and the increased importance of the tail as a fluke. The cord displays a

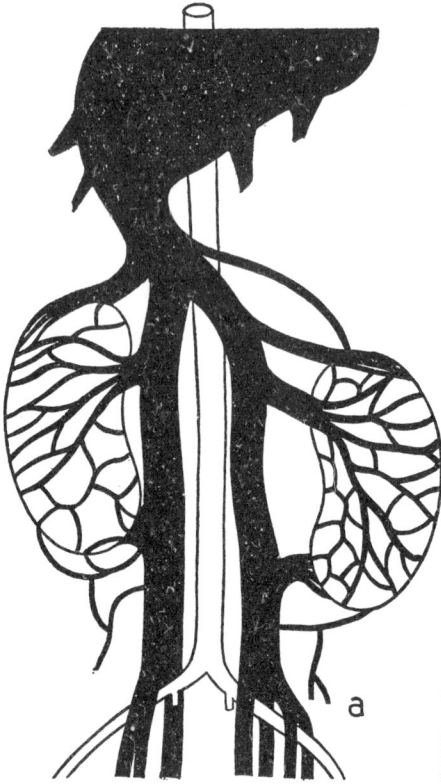

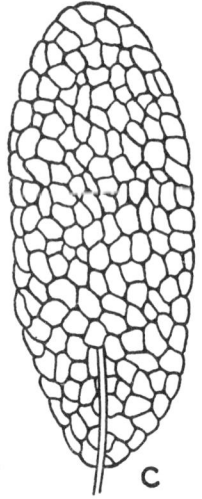

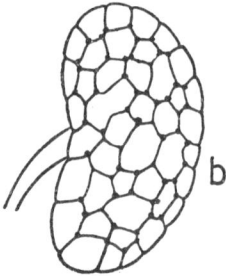

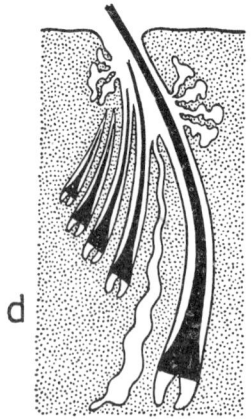

marked cervical enlargement but only a slight lumbar one. The cell groups in the lumbar region that would normally innervate the hind limb are absent as are those in the cervical region that would supply muscles of the hand. The motor cell columns in the thoracic and lumbar regions show considerable complexity in their arrangement, probably a direct response to the muscular complexity associated with development of the flukes.

REPRODUCTION

It is not so difficult a problem to determine reproductive patterns in laboratory animals, but with cetaceans the matter is by no means easy and there are still many mysteries. Only when many more observations have been made on material from a much wider range of species and on animals kept in captivity will answers be found to several perplexing problems. Nothing is known at all about reproductive events in many cetacean species either because of lack of specimens or because so few have been obtained at important times in their cycles.

The age at reaching puberty is known only for a few species and even then the ages given are probably not exact. Usually the larger whales attain puberty later than the smaller ones. Blue Whales are thought to be able to reproduce when over six years old and similar figures have been given for Fin, Sei and Humpback Whales. White Whales and some other dolphins mature some time between five and six years and porpoises at over three years, possibly older still: our specimens suggest that reproduction in some species occurs after the sixth year[33]. The life span of cetaceans is extremely difficult to assess. There are several interesting

---

Fig. 5. Seal venous system. Kidneys. Hair follicles
  a Diagram of the abdominal venous system in a phocid
  b Outline of a seal kidney
  c Outline of a cetacean kidney
  d Sketch of the hair follicles and associated glands in a seal

methods available, but none is conclusive. Counting
the scars of corpora lutea[50] in the ovaries gives an indication of the number of ovulations and as in many cetaceans
these scars persist apparently for the animal's lifetime
the count could be significant if the pattern of reproductive events were known and if every ovulation were
followed by pregnancy. Periodicity in the formation of
baleen[67] has already been mentioned (p. 51) as the basis
of a method for ageing. Investigation of the rate of deposition of layers of dentine[69] has helped to assess age in
odontocetes and sectioning of the 'wax plug' found in the
deeper part of the external auditory meatus of mysticetes
has revealed incremental rings[64]. The rings appear to be
related to the increase in size of the skull and thus of the
meatus resulting in the addition of layers of cornified
epithelium to the plug. It is likely, however, that all these
periodic markings and rings in baleen, dentine and plugs
are affected by metabolic and other activities. Not surprisingly there is often little correlation between any two
methods. From their application, however, it has been
estimated probably with much variation that the largest
mysticetes and odontocetes have a life span of up to 80
years, that Narwhals, Killer and Pilot Whales live for about
40 years and that dolphins survive for little over 25 years.

The information available about the reproductive pattern
in each cetacean species varies in amount and in accuracy[54].
Blue Whales mate in June and July, winter months in the
southern hemisphere, give birth about 11 months later and
have a lactation period of about 6 months. There is thus
a minimum interval between successive births of two years
and a female reaching an age of thirty could presumably
have given birth to twelve offspring during her lifetime if
each mating were followed by conception. Twinning is rare
in cetaceans, though multiple births of up to six have been
recorded: the incidence of twins in Blue Whales is slightly
over 0·6 per cent. A newborn Blue Whale calf is about
8 m long, weighs 2,000 kg and is able to swim actively
from birth. Sperm Whales mate from September to Decem-

ber in the southern hemisphere and give birth to a single calf 15–16 months later. Lactation lasts about a year. The shortest gestation period, of about 8 months, is found in porpoises which, with a lactation period of about 6 months, can give birth to young each year. It seems that many cetaceans have a limited mating season, though some, such as Narwhals, Pilot and Killer Whales, can breed throughout the year but have several months with maximum mating intensity. The Sei Whale has a feeding migration to the south in the southern summer and a breeding migration northwards in the winter. Mating and parturition take place in tropical and sub-tropical waters: lactation is usually over by the time the southern feeding grounds are reached. It has been considered that ovulation occurs once during the mating season, but evidence is accumulating that Blue, Humpback and Sperm Whales are polyoestrous and can ovulate several times before fertilization occurs[54,55]. It has proved difficult to tell the difference between corpora albicantia of the oestrous cycles and those of pregnancy. Thus, even if the corpora do persist for very long periods, as they do in Baleen Whales, there is as yet no absolutely certain method of identifying the history and significance of each corpus and thus of accurately ageing whales by this method. Indeed one of us[6,32] found the corpora albicantia in the ovaries of the apparently polyoestrous Pilot Whale eventually retrogress to become invisible to the naked eye. The corpus luteum of pregnancy certainly persists throughout the gestation period in all species examined so far, and can be over 4 kg in weight in large whales, but it retrogresses steadily after birth to become a small corpus albicans.

Mating in all cetaceans occurs in the water and is generally believed to be of short duration. Although all authorities comment on the amorousness and tender courtship behaviour of many cetaceans, mating has seldom been observed. Humpbacks have been seen to dive, approach each other at speed to turn upwards vertically and copulate with ventral surfaces apposed, surfacing as they do so and emerging from the sea as far as their abdomens. This is immediately followed by the pairing couple falling back into the sea with a resounding slap that is loud enough to make intrepid explorers nearby think the ice is breaking up beneath them. Mating can also occur with the pair swimming horizontally side by side, the male easing his body slightly arched and on his side beneath the raised abdomen of the female. Such alleged mating behaviour has been seen among dolphins captive in oceanaria where intergeneric copulation has occurred between Bottlenosed males and females of the Pacific Striped Dolphin (*L. obliquidens*). It is not known whether these intergeneric matings occur in the wild, or if they are ever fertile, though it has been suggested that certain skeletons of dolphins look like crosses between two other not unrelated forms. Observation of captive dolphins has revealed a pronounced libido in their sexual behaviour. They enjoy playing and rubbing on ropes or other available projections, attempt to copulate with turtles, or fish and have even embarrassed divers by their approaches. It must be remembered that males in fact use their penis almost as a finger in their investigations of anything curious, thus their overtures are not always sexual in intent. Weddell has shown that the external genitalia are profusely innervated with sensory end organs.

There is no evidence that any cetacean displays delayed implantation (see p. 142). There is, however, at least as far as the accuracy of the records allows, not such a striking difference in the length of gestation as the birth weights might suggest. A Blue Whale at birth weighs 2,000 kg whereas a newborn porpoise weighs little more than 10 kg, yet the gestation period of a Blue Whale is only a few weeks longer than that of a porpoise. It is during the fifth to eighth month of pregnancy that the foetal growth rate[49] increases rapidly, to up to ten times that of some other mammals, and this is a period when abundant food supplies are available for Blue Whale cows. It seems that there is a specific foetal growth rate for each cetacean species, and that all species develop at rates different from those of other mammals.

Birth[71] takes place under water and has only been seen in dolphins in captivity or in Rorquals killed while in labour. The great majority of births occur fluke first: the umbilical cord snaps close to the umbilicus and the newborn calf either swims to the surface or is pushed up by its mother or another cow. Dolphins can swim immediately they are born and surface within a few seconds of birth, the contact of air on the skin being the stimulus to initiate respiration. Should the umbilical cord not break at birth the placenta is pulled out by the calf and may prevent the calf surfacing to breathe. It is not known whether the cow ever bites through the cord and there is no evidence that the cow ever eats the placenta. Most observers state that the placenta is shed after a pause of several hours.

Accounts of the cetacean placenta are mostly fragmentary because of the difficulty in obtaining well-fixed material, the time lapse between death and removal of the tissue often being many hours. The size of the uterus also often precludes reasonable preservation. It is therefore not surprising that we know most about the placenta of dolphins[78], though from all appearances it seems that the organ in other cetaceans has a similar gross arrangement. The foetus is usually found in the left horn of the bicornuate uterus in odontocetes (80 per cent), but in mysticetes the pregnancy has been found in the right horn in 60 per cent of whales examined. The chorionic sac extends into the opposite horn which also contains a prolongation of the large allantois. The umbilical cord contains two large arteries and two large veins: these pair off and from where the cord divides extend in opposite directions along the mesometrial border of the allantois branching frequently to vascularise the chorion. The cord also contains the allantoic duct and sometimes numerous serous clefts or spaces, regarded by some as lymphatics, but which are more likely to be residual remnants of the exocoelome. Both the cord and the inner aspect of the amnion bear numerous pearl-like epithelial plaques similar to those seen in ungulates. The cord has also been reported to contain occasional bundles of smooth muscle scattered throughout the stroma.

The thin chorion, lined by the allantois throughout its extent except where the amnion comes between it and the allantois at the antimesometrial aspect of the pregnant horn, is much pleated and is covered with villous processes. The pleats and villi fit into corresponding depressions and crypts on the internal surface of the uterine mucosa which has a rugose appearance. The degree of complexity of the folds and their intimacy of interdigitation varies in different parts of the uterus. At the extremities of each horn and along much of the mesometrial border the folding of the mucosa is very marked and gives a sponge-like appearance. These regions have been likened by Wislocki to the placentomes of ungulates in which numerous branching chorionic villi fit into complex crypts of the cushion-like maternal caruncle. It is impossible, even by manipulation, to separate the chorion from the uterine mucosa in these placentomatous regions so freely interlocked are the villi and crypts. Elsewhere in the horn villi are interlocked within crypts but the folding is much less complex and spongy. On the antimesometrial aspect there are only short villi and the chorion is relatively avascular as opposed to its marked vascularity elsewhere. The region within the pregnant horn where the surfaces of allantois and amnion fuse back to back is membranous and totally avascular.

The chorionic villi are stout with a central core of well vascularized connective tissue. They are covered by a single layer of low columnar (trophoblast) cells with distinct cell boundaries. Several authors have described a brush border to the chorionic cells which may well turn out to be made of microvilli or cytoplasmic projections. No giant or binucleate cells have been observed and the presence of intraepithelial capillaries has been questioned except in *Globicephala*[2]. There is indeed an abundant plexus of capillaries everywhere beneath the trophoblast cells but none actually penetrates the covering epithelial layer. The trophoblast cells often appear vacuolated but the significance of these usually large vacuoles is unknown. The maternal crypts are everywhere lined by a continuous layer of flattened epithelial cells beneath which are numerous maternal capillaries. There is doubt as to whether these cells are in the form of a syncytium or discrete and separate: only electron microscopy of well-fixed material will decide. The uterine glands appear to be active during pregnancy and to deliver their secretion into the bases of the maternal crypts where the degree of fusion of foetal and maternal epithelia is not as intimate, thereby allowing uterine secretions to be absorbed by the trophoblast. The cetacean placenta is thus diffuse and epitheliochorial and there would seem to be no particular features that can be associated with life in the sea or with diving mechanisms (see p. 148).

Inspection of sections of small pieces of placenta of the large mysticetes confirms much that is stated above about appearances in the odontocete placenta. There are, however, areas of trophoblast in the bases of deep maternal crypts where the cells are tall and columnar and arranged in large groups, almost in a 'rosette' fashion as seen in those structures in the porcine placenta. This would suggest that these rosettes are particularly engaged in absorbing and possibly storing nutriment from the uterine secretions. The maternal epithelium becomes much thinned on the summits of the uterine ridges, so marked in places is the attenuation that it seems probable that some attrition of the layer occurs in these regions, a state of affairs almost universal in ungulate placentomes. The cetacean placenta is thus quite unlike that of pinnipeds (p. 148) and bears some distinct relationships with that of ungulates.

One striking feature of the female reproductive tract of many cetaceans is the presence of several folds in the upper part of the vagina[32]. These lie immediately caudal to what may be considered the true cervix. They have a valve-like arrangement and create an upper dilatation of the vagina into a 'spermathecal' recess (Fig. 4). It has been suggested that the valves prevent semen seeping back into the sea after withdrawal of the penis. It seems unlikely that the penis is inserted beyond the hindermost fold and as both

4

the vaginal walls and its folds are very muscular it is possible valve-like disposition enables the folds to act as a pump. All the vaginal folds, the cervical canal and the walls of the uterine horns exhibit a series of longitudinal ridges. The changes in the uterine mucosa of Balaenopterid whales during the reproductive cycle are striking[57]. Crypt formation begins immediately after ovulation but the greatest degree of complexity reached by branched dendritic processes on the surface of the stratum compactum of the uterine mucosa is only reached at the end of pregnancy. Post-partum involution is rapid and the separation of placental tissue at birth and the degeneration of any that remains in the crypts is accomplished without damage to the uterine mucosa and without any loss of maternal blood.

Most odontocetes suckle their calves for about a year: lactation in the largest mysticetes is seldom longer than 6 month's duration and its length appears to be related to the availability of krill. Suckling always takes place under water, the young approaching the slow-swimming mother from the rear. As the mother can remain submerged for longer than her calf it means that the calf has to surface frequently during suckling and young dolphins can only remain at the nipple for quite short periods. The calf presses on the sides of the mammary slit with its mouth and the nipple becomes protruded between the calf's tongue and palate. Myo-epithelial cells, of which there are many surrounding the lobules of the mammary glands, contract during suckling and cause milk to spurt freely into the throat of the calf. It is not yet known how much milk each cetacean calf obtains at each suckling period, though it must be measured in gallons in large Rorquals. Whale milk is thick, creamy and concentrated. It contains about 50 per cent of fat, 10–12 per cent of protein but only 2 per cent of sugar. This means that the calf need not be suckled for as long at each suckling period as a land mammal to obtain the same quantity of foodstuffs. The concentrated milk also enables the mother to conserve water and at the same time to provide her young with milk of the highly nutritious quality necessary for rapid growth. Fats, too, liberate much water when metabolized, another advantage to a marine mammal.

5

Seals, Sea Lions and Walruses

The Pinnipedia includes the seals, sea lions, fur seals and walruses[1,9,15]. Some of these are from their frequent appearances in circuses and zoos well known animals, but some have been seen only rarely and are little known. As their name indicates, Pinnipedia—from the Latin *pinna* (or *penna*), a feather, and *pes*, a foot—they all possess the modification of their limbs for swimming, a first requisite for an aquatic mammal. The bones of the limbs are short and almost completely withdrawn into the body, leaving the flippers protruding. The digits are connected together with a web of skin, presenting an increased surface area to the water. As well as bringing the source of power nearer to the body, the lack of long 'terrestrial' limbs means that the animal is more streamlined. The streamlining effect is to be found all over the body, the smooth rounded head, with no long external ears, passes without a definite break into the trunk, which, while it may be plump and rounded, or sinuous and elongated, is without sharp protuberances. The smooth contour is assisted by the layer of blubber under the skin and the fusiform body ends in a small tail which fits neatly between the hind flippers.

There are three main divisions of the Order (Fig. 6): the true or 'earless' seals (Phocidae); the sea lions and fur seals, also known as 'eared' seals (Otariidae), and the walruses (Odobenidae). The true seals are easily distinguishable as their flippers have hair on all surfaces, and their hind flippers are stretched backwards, soles opposed and cannot be brought forwards beneath the body. They cannot, therefore, take any of the body weight, so that on land the seals progress by wriggling or sliding movements. There is no obvious external pinna. The eared seals, or otaries, are able to turn their hind flippers forwards and walk, rather than wriggle, on land and both fore and hind flippers have naked black palms and soles. They have an inch long, furled and pointed external ear pinna. Walruses are able to move their hind flippers as can otaries, but lack the ear pinna.

Compared with other groups in the animal kingdom the number of genera of seals is small, and many contain only a single species[1,9,15]. There are five genera of living sea lions, two fur seal genera, a single genus for walruses, and thirteen phocid genera (see p. 102). Some account of the relationships of these seals will be mentioned, although it is not relevant here to go into the reasons for their detailed classification, many of which involve small differences of skull morphology.

The taxonomic history[1] of the pinnipeds stretches from the classification of Linnaeus in 1758, *Phoca* being the only one of his generic names still standing (although not with precisely the same meaning), to the latest specific epithet *insularis* (now in the Common Seal synonymy) created as recently as 1964. But the knowledge and history of the animals themselves go, of course, much further back. Drawings of seals on pieces of reindeer antler have been found from Palaeolithic times, and the Neolithic Scandinavians hunted seals, carved their bones into harpoon heads and used their teeth as a decorative fringe for cloaks. Monk Seals were known to the poets and writers of classical Greece. A good description was given by Aristotle (384–322 BC), and they were mentioned by Pliny (AD 61–113). They were also included in an inventory of 1341 of the Canary Islands, and there are records from 1434 when the industrial exploitation of Monk Seals near Cap Blanc is said to have started. Books, often large, and frequently incredibly and entertainingly illustrated by artists, who had certainly never seen some of the animals, were written on marine creatures in the sixteenth century. In many of these, such as Rondoletius (1554), Olaus Magnus (1555) and Gesner (1558), the seals were included amongst the fish. During the seventeenth and eighteenth centuries descriptions, often in Latin, of general internal and external anatomy were published: a German scholar in 1683 aspiring to a higher degree with just such a paper.

Whenever seals were known, they played a large part in the lives of the coastal natives, who soon had legends about them. As well as being used for clothing, a seal skin drawn round a field would protect it from hailstones while the clothing would protect the owner from lightning, and insomnia could be cured by a seal's flipper placed under the pillow at night. Bering Strait Eskimoes believed that the souls of seals remained with their urinary bladders, and that by returning these to the sea, the souls joined fresh bodies that could, in their turn, be hunted.

CLASSIFICATION

Order Pinnipedia
  Superfamily Otarioidea
    Family Odobenidae
            Odobenus—walrus

    Family Otariidae
      Subfamily Otariinae
            Otaria—Southern Sea Lion
            Eumetopias—Northern or Steller's Sea Lion
            Neophoca—Australian Sea Lion
            Phocarctos—Hooker's Sea Lion
            Zalophus—Californian Sea Lion

      Subfamily Arctocephalinae
            Callorhinus—Pribilof or Alaska Fur Seal
            Arctocephalus—Southern Fur Seals

  Superfamily Phocoidea
    Family Phocidae
      Subfamily Phocinae
        Tribe Erignathini
            Erignathus—Bearded Seal
        Tribe Cystophorini
            Cystophora—Hooded Seal

Tribe Phocini
  Subtribe Phocina
     Halichoerus—Grey Seal
     Phoca—Common Seal
     Pusa—Ringed, Baikal and Caspian Seals
     Pagophilus—Greenland or Harp Seal
     Histriophoca—Ribbon or Banded Seal
Subfamily Monachinae
  Tribe Monachini
     Monachus—Monk Seals
  Tribe Lobodontini
     Lobodon—Crabeater Seal
     Leptonychotes—Weddell Seal
     Hydrurga—Leopard Seal
     Ommatophoca—Ross Seal
     Mirounga—Elephant Seal

RELATIONSHIPS AND FOSSILS

According to different textbooks, the Pinnipedia are variously regarded as a full Order, or else as a suborder of the Order Carnivora[102]. Recent work on the fossil history of the group suggests that the latter arrangement may be the better one.

The division of the Order into three families, the Otariidae, Odobenidae and Phocidae presents no difficulties, but the origin of all these families is not yet absolutely clear as the fossil record has not yet given up all its secrets. Four interrelated groups tell us the story of otarioid seals.[121] The first and earliest of these is the Enaliarctidae—the ancestral group—from which the other three groups could have been derived. The ancestral enaliarctids came from Californian deposits of about 22·5 million years old—from the beginning of the Miocene. The skull fragments had carnassial teeth—thus indicating that they belonged to the Order Carnivora; they also had resemblances to ursids, and to otarioids, and some characters indicated aquatic specialization. Because of their aquatic specializations these animals were not ursids, yet because they still had carnassials they were not yet otarioids, and their feet show pinniped characters. Their origin from a terrestrial ursid subfamily is accepted, and they are regarded as a separate family of proto-otarioids.

The Desmatophocidae diverged from this ancestral group in the early Miocene; they became specialized and had typical pinniped flippers but did not give rise to any modern groups and became extinct in the late Miocene. They lived in the coastal waters of the north Pacific.

Walruses probably originated along the Californian coast, the earliest one so far known being from the middle Miocene some 14 million years ago. One group—the Dusignathinae, developed their upper and lower canines to about the same size. Several genera of these early walruses evolved, and they were the dominant seals of the north Pacific for about 5 million years, though they became extinct about 14 million years ago. Walruses of the subfamily Odobeninae developed their upper canines and reduced the lower ones, as in modern forms. The first of these true walruses is known from the late Miocene (6·5 million years ago) of Mexico. All other later odobenine fossils are known only from the north Atlantic and it is possible that an early walrus migrated into the Atlantic through the seaway between North and South America. From the Pleistocene onwards all walruses belong to the modern genus *Odobenus*.

Probably about 14 million years ago the otariid seals developed from the ancestral group. *Arctocephalus* is probably the genus most like the original ancestral otariid, and small size and a thick undercoat of fur are considered as being primitive characters. From the primitive fur seal line developed *Callorhinus*, all the species of *Arctocephalus*, and, probably as recently as 3 million years ago, the sea lion genera. Fur seals and sea lions dispersed from their area of origin in the north Pacific and became widely distributed in the southern hemisphere, though none of these animals has yet reached the north Atlantic.

The origin of phocid seals took place around the margins of the north Atlantic, probably about the beginning of the

Miocene (20 million years ago)[118]. Even then the Phocinae and the Monachinae were separate groups, representatives of both subfamilies being present on both sides of the north Atlantic. Relatively little is known yet about the evolution of the phocine seals. *Pusa* is mentioned on p. 111. Apparently the phocines reacted to the poor climate of the Pliocene by adaptation, and the modern animals began to appear. It seems that many of these phocines were late in appearance and may well still be evolving rapidly.

Monachine seals seem to have been the dominant seals of the Pliocene north Atlantic. The west Atlantic common ancestor of Monk Seals and Elephant Seals passed through the Central American Seaway, to diverge into modern forms; the east Atlantic Monk Seal entered the Mediterranean; and monachines dispersed to Argentina and South Africa. Eventually these southern hemisphere forms gave rise to the modern Antarctic seals but little is known about this yet.

Characters of the teeth and carpal bones indicate that both otarioids and phocoids have come from the Carnivora. The fine details of the tympanic bulla show that pinnipeds have affinities with the Canoidea, rather than the Felodea, and with the arctoid canoids rather than with the canids. The ear region of seals shows many aquatic specializations, and if these are metaphorically 'removed', the primitive relationships can be seen. Otarioid seals show their affinities with an Oligocene ursid subfamily, while the ear region of phocids is like that of early mustelids. Pinnipeds thus show a dual origin from two different groups of arctoid carnivores[79,115,123].

LIVING SEALS OF THE WORLD

Seals are found chiefly in Arctic and Antarctic seas and adjacent cooler waters, the elongation of their ranges farther afield following quite closely the cold ocean currents. It is not practicable to deal in too much detail with each species, but a brief account of each one will be given here; the world, for this purpose being divided into Arctic, cool north, cool south, and Antarctic[1,9,15].

Seals from Arctic waters

In the Arctic the most common seal is the small 1·5 m Ringed Seal (*Pusa hispida*), so called because of the dark ring-like markings on its grey coat. It is found wherever there is open water amongst the ice, and may extend as far as the North Pole. Six geographical subspecies have been described, one reaching Japan, one in the Baltic, and two from fresh-water lakes in Finland. Keeping closer to the coasts of the Arctic Ocean are the Bearded Seals (*Erignathus barbatus*) with their abundant bristly moustaches. In the northern Pacific and Bering Sea is the Banded Seal (*Histriophoca fasciata*), one of the few seals to have a strikingly patterned coat. The chocolate brown coat of the male has a wide creamy band round the neck, the hind end of the body and round the base of each fore flipper. Females are similarly patterned but paler. This distribution of colour makes the coat too difficult to be used commercially. Although the seals are not specifically hunted, some are taken by the Japanese and included with the Common Seals for oil, meat and leather. Little is known about Banded Seals, and their total numbers have been estimated as about 40,000. In the northern Atlantic from Novaya Zemlya to Greenland and Newfoundland is found the Harp Seal (*Pagophilus groenlandicus*). The adult male is a light grey with a black horseshoe-shaped band on the back, and a black head. Three main populations of this seal have distinct breeding grounds, in the White Sea, near Jan Mayen and near Newfoundland. The thick white coat of the young pup is the object of commercial hunting.

One of the largest (3 m) and most distinctive of the Arctic seals is the Hooded Seal (*Cystophora cristata*) which lives in the deep water and on the drifting ice from Spitsbergen to Iceland, southern Greenland and Labrador. These big seals, dark grey blotched with black, have as their most noticeable character an enlargement of the nasal cavity in the adult males. This hood or crest, from which the animal takes its name, is a bladder-like structure on the top of the head, which hangs down in front of the mouth when relaxed, and is blown up in times of anger. Another curious feature of this seal is the red balloon-shaped extrusion of the very pliable membranous internasal septum, which it is able to blow out through one nostril, but whose function is unknown.

The best known pinniped of the Arctic regions is the large and unmistakable walrus (Fig. 6). Divided into two subspecies, the Atlantic Walrus[116] (*Odobenus rosmarus rosmarus*) occurs from the Barrow Strait to Baffin Island and west Greenland, and from Iceland and Spitsbergen to the Barents and Kara Seas, while the Pacific Walrus[85] (*O.r. divergens*) is found in the Bering Sea, and eastwards to Point Barrow, and westwards to the Laptev Sea where its range comes very close to that of the Atlantic animal. Walruses prefer shallow water round the coasts, and rarely go far out to sea. The big adult male may be 4 m in length and weigh up to 1,500 kg, while the females are slightly smaller. They have rough, warty skin, sparsely covered with reddish hair, a big display of quill-like whiskers, and the characteristic tusks are present in both sexes. Walrus pups have been frequently reared in captivity and proved to be most friendly, engaging and entertaining creatures.

Seals of the cool north
No other seal of the northern hemisphere is found in really Arctic waters. The most northerly otariid is the Pribilof Fur Seal (*Callorhinus ursinus*) which forms large breeding rookeries on the Pribilof and Commander Islands, in the eastern and western Bering Sea respectively, and on Robben Island off Sakhalin. Large numbers of these fur seals migrate south during the spring and summer, reaching the shores of Japan at about 35°N, and as far as San Diego, California, before returning north. The longer dark brown guard hairs of the fur seals conceal the shorter, finer, very abundant chestnut coloured underfur hairs, which give 'fur

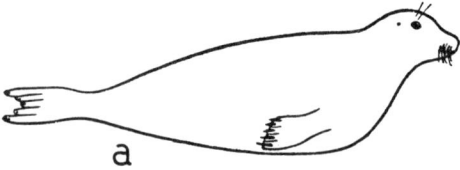

a

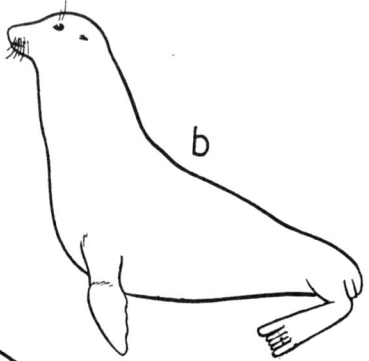

b

c

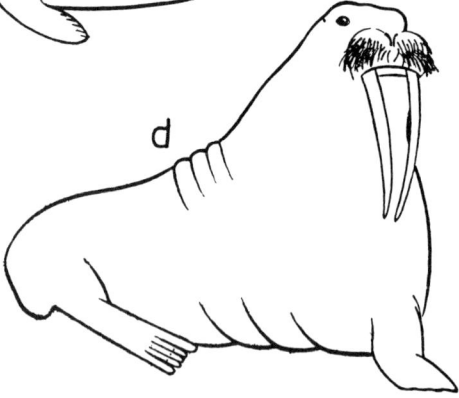

d

seals' their name and make the animals the object of much commercial hunting. The only other fur seal which occurs north of the Equator is the Guadalupe Fur Seal (*Arctocephalus townsendi*) found on Guadalupe off Lower California. For historical reasons the more southerly Juan Fernandez Fur Seal (*A. philippii*) and the Galapagos Fur Seal (*A. galapagoensis*) will also be mentioned here. *A. townsendi* and *A. philippii* are closely related, and *A. galapagoensis*, a small animal, is more closely related to the South American Fur Seal (*A. australis*). At the end of the eighteenth century all these fur seals were present in enormous numbers, but the millions of skins taken during sealing reduced them to near extinction. Miraculously, a few seals survived and the populations are recovering now, but the small colonies were only recently rediscovered in the 1950s[99]. At the present time each population of these three recovering colonies numbers about 500–1,000 seals.

The two sea lions of the north are Steller's (*Eumetopias jubatus*) and the Californian Sea Lion (*Zalophus californianus*). The former occurs on both sides of the Pacific from Japan to California, the Aleutian Islands possessing the greatest abundance of breeding colonies, although others are found off the coasts of Kamchatka, Alaska and British Columbia. The 3 m long adult males, 1,000 kg in weight, develop a coarse mane of hair about their necks. The females are smaller (2·5 m), and both sexes are a golden-brown colour. Although these sea lions are of less commercial value than they used to be when the Aleutian natives made much use of their skins, the meat is still sold to mink farms. The Californian Sea Lion is perhaps the best known of all pinnipeds (Fig. 6). This lithe, chocolate-brown animal can climb steps, balance balls on its nose

Fig. 6. Examples of living pinnipeds
    a Common Seal (*Phoca vitulina*)
    b Californian Sea Lion (*Zalophus californianus*)
    c Southern Elephant Seal (*Mirounga leonina*)
    d Walrus (*Odobenus rosmarus*)

while doing so and be taught to play a tune on a row of motor horns. It is remembered by children all over the world from its catching ability at feeding time in zoos, and from the way in circuses it can applaud its friends by clapping its flippers. Only recently it has been shown to possess methods of echo locating not unlike those used by bats and cetaceans. Populations of this sea lion are found off the Californian coast and on the Galapagos Islands. Those on the Galapagos are slightly smaller and sometimes given a separate subspecific name. There is no information about the state of the Japanese population.

All other seals of the temperate north are phocids. The two that live round British coasts are the Grey (*Halichoerus grypus*) and the Common or Harbour Seals (*Phoca vitulina*). The Grey Seal, an inhabitant of rocky shores, has large breeding colonies on North Rona and the Orkneys, and at suitable, secluded parts of the west coast down to the Scilly Islands and round the Irish coast. There is also a colony on the Farne Islands, and a growing one off Great Yarmouth[84]. A few individuals have explored the Wash, but as yet there are no breeding colonies there. There is an extension of the range to Iceland, the Norwegian coast, and the neck of the White Sea. A second, distinct population lives in the Baltic, and a third in the Gulf of St Lawrence. There is mixing of these populations while at sea, but they tend to return to their own breeding grounds. On our shores Grey and Common Seals are sometimes confused, but the greater size (3 m) and high, arched 'Roman' nose of the adult male, and the more parallel nostrils of the Grey Seal distinguish it from the Common Seal which is smaller (2 m) with a rounder, more cat-like head and nostrils that have their lower ends closer together and thus form a V. The Common Seal is an animal of estuaries and sandbanks (Fig. 6). The distribution, on both sides of both Atlantic and Pacific Oceans, is marked by its subdivision into six subspecies. In the eastern Atlantic it occurs from Iceland to the Netherlands and Germany, from the Shetlands to the Wash, Bristol Channel and Ireland. On the American side its chief range is from southern Greenland to Maine. In the eastern Pacific it is common in the estuaries of the Alaskan to the Californian coasts, and in the west, from the Bering Sea to Japan. In this latter area there are two subspecies, one breeding on rocky islets and one being associated with pack ice[122]. A landlocked group is found in the Upper and Lower Seal Lakes on the east side of the Hudson Bay.

The only other lake seals are the small (1·5 m) Caspian (*Pusa caspica*) and Baikal Seals (*Pusa sibirica*), in the lakes, or inland seas, from which they take their names. Both animals are related to the Ringed Seal (p. 106), the Baikal Seal probably more closely than the Caspian. While the Paratethyan Sea was isolated from the north Atlantic in late Miocene times, the phocids that had entered Paratethys earlier were unable to escape, and they continued evolving there in isolation. The ringed Seal *Pusa* probably developed here and eventually gave origin to the Baikal and Caspian Seals. Later, the Ringed Seal invaded the Arctic seas from Paratethys, and the Baikal and Caspian Seals remained isolated in their respective bodies of fresh water[118].

The Monk Seals[103] are a little known group, the three species widely separated, and in the warmer regions of the world. The Mediterranean Monk Seal (*Monachus monachus*) occurs in the Black Sea, in the less populous parts of the Mediterranean, and down the western coasts of Africa as far as Cap Blanc. The West Indian Monk Seal (*Monachus tropicalis*), although caught for oil in the eighteenth century, is most probably extinct today. The Laysan Seal[102] (*Monachus schauinslandi*), although living on remote coral atolls in the western end of the Hawaiian chain, is probably the best known of the three because of the interest taken in it by zoologists attached to the U.S. Navy which administers a base there. The three Monk Seals are similar in many respects but there are sufficient differences in their skulls and teeth, even apart from their distribution, for them to be regarded as separate species.

The remaining phocid of the northern hemisphere is the

Northern Elephant Seal[81] (*Mirounga angustirostris*) which lives on islands off the coast of Mexico and southern California. In most respects it is very similar to its southern counterpart, and the peculiarities of elephant seals will be mentioned later (p. 115). Certain skull and behavioural differences, and the slightly different shape of the proboscis show that the two species are separate. The Northern Elephant Seal is also more placid and does not seem to have the ability to bend its back directly backwards so that its head touches its back, as its southern relative can.

Seals of the southern hemisphere

The seals of the more temperate seas of the southern hemisphere are all otariids. The Australasian region houses two sea lions, both of restricted distribution. The Australian Sea Lion (*Neophoca cinerea*) lives mainly on offshore islands of South and Western Australia from Kangaroo Island to Houtmans Abrolhos. The big adult male (2 m) is blackish with a cream nape and top to its head; the females are grey dorsally and cream ventrally. The main breeding colony on Dangerous Reef, S.A., has about 200 animals[114]. Hooker's Sea Lion (*Phocarctos hookeri*) breeds on the Auckland Islands and Campbell Island south of New Zealand, although it may wander as far as Macquarie Island where individual animals have been seen several years in succession. The Southern Sea Lion[89,117] (*Otaria byronia*) occurs on the rocky offshore islands off Uruguay and Argentina, and probably along the southern Peruvian coast as well, although little is known of them there. There is a large population (400,000) on the Falkland Islands.

The fur seals of the southern hemisphere are widely distributed animals, some well known because of their commercial importance, others hardly known at all. They vary between 2·0 and 3·0 m in length, those of South Africa and Australia being the largest. All are approximately similar in colour, a blackish brown with chestnut underfur, the males with a thick mane. The South American Fur Seal (*Arctocephalus australis*) occurs from Rio de Janeiro to

SEALS, SEA LIONS AND WALRUSES

Peru, in very much the same places as the Southern Sea Lion, although the latter prefer the sandy beaches, while the fur seals like rocky places. There are colonies of about 14,000 animals on the Falkland Islands, perhaps 4,000–5,000 in Peru, and the largest numbers, of about 56,000 seals, are to be found in Uruguay. The number of animals seems to be about static at the moment. Only the Uruguayan herds are exploited, about 5,000 seals being taken annually for fur, meat meal and oil. The South African Fur Seal (*Arctocephalus pusillus pusillus*), whose biology is well known because of its commercial importance for blubber and fur, occurs off the coast of South Africa from Cape Cross to Algoa Bay. It is the most abundant of the southern fur seals, with a population estimated at about 500,000 animals. The Kerguelen Fur Seal (*Arctocephalus gazella*) lives on remote islands south of the Antarctic Convergence*[104]. It occurs on Kerguelen, Heard, Bouvet, South Georgia, South Shetlands and South Orkneys. Remarkable recoveries have been made after near extinction by the sealers, and now the main population of some 70,000 is on South Georgia. On islands north of the Convergence—Tristan, Gough, Marion, St Paul and Amsterdam—the Amsterdam Island Fur Seal (*A. tropicalis*) occurs, and the total population of this seal has recovered to about 20,000 animals. The Australian Fur Seal (*Arctocephalus pusillus doriferus*) is not demonstrably different from the South African Fur Seal and is given subspecific status only[120]. It lives on the offshore islands of southern New South Wales, Victoria and Tasmania, with Victoria having the greatest colonies of over 12,000 seals. The New Zealand Fur Seal (*A. forsteri*) is found on many of the exposed rocky parts of South Island, and on the neighbouring islands—Macquarie, Campbell, Bounty, Chatham and Auckland. It also occurs in Australian waters on offshore islands of Western Australia to Kangaroo Island[107], South Australia. The other species of *Arctocephalus* are

*Antarctic Convergence[53]—a boundary line round the southern hemisphere indicating where the cold Antarctic water sinks below the warmer sub-Antarctic water.

mentioned on p. 109. There has been doubt as to whether all these fur seals are, in fact, distinct but differences in the size of the skull and in the shape of the teeth make all the species distinguishable.

Seals of the Antarctic

The Antarctic seals are all phocids. Apart from the Southern Elephant Seal[110,111,112] (*Mirounga leonina*) which belongs to the sub-Antarctic islands, the other four species, related to each other, are found within reach of the ice. The most northerly of the four, and the largest, is the 3·5 m Leopard Seal (*Hydrurga leptonyx*) which lives in the outer fringes of the pack ice and may move to the sub-Antarctic islands in the winter. The name comes from the colour of their coat—grey spotted with black, and has no connection with their temperament. They are quite inoffensive, usually solitary, animals, dangerous, unless molested, only to penguins and other prey, but they have acquired a quite undeservedly sinister reputation, possibly because of the long, slim body with its large head which has a curiously reptilian appearance, and the impressive teeth with their three long cusps. The Crabeater[82] (*Lobodon carcinophagus*) is probably the most abundant seal of the Antarctic, and although its habitat makes an accurate count impossible, there are probably up to about 5,000,000 of these seals. They are pelagic, gregarious animals, found and moving with the drifting pack ice round the Antarctic continent. Their cheek teeth are characteristic and peculiar, the recurved cusps fitting nicely together when the jaws are closed to form a sieve through which the shrimp-like krill are separated from the water (Fig. 4). They are also known as White Seals because during the summer the silvery grey coat fades quickly to a creamy white.

The 3 m Ross Seal[106] (*Ommatophoca rossi*) lives, usually singly, in the heavier pack ice farther south. It has been seen only a relatively small number of times and few specimens have been collected, so that many of its details are unknown. Its small head, plump body and well developed flippers indicate that it is a fast swimmer, and its enormous eyes suggest a fine perception of movement, particularly, perhaps, of the squid on which it feeds. It is said to make curious cooing noises, using its long soft palate as a resonator. Most southerly of all is the Weddell Seal[82,109] (*Leptonychotes weddelli*) It is found close to the Antarctic continent, within sight of land, and not on the pack ice. The coat, blackish dorsally and whitish ventrally, fades to a rusty colour during the summer, but never reaches the paleness of the Crabeater. When on the ice, their habit of sleeping on their sides makes them easily recognizable.

The Southern Elephant Seal[86,110-112] (*Mirounga leonina*) is found on most of the sub-Antarctic islands, and breeding colonies occur off Argentine, from South Georgia to the South Shetland Islands, and on the Falkland, Gough, Marion, Crozet, Kerguelen, Heard, Macquarie and Campbell Islands. Individual animals may wander as far as Australia and South Africa. These are the largest of the Pinnipedia, the adult males reaching up to 6·5 m in length, and the females up to 3·5 m (Fig. 6). Adult males have thick, rough skin on their chests caused by the scar tissue of numerous fights, but their most characteristic feature is the inflatable nasal sac, which is not present in females. It is an enlargement of the nasal cavity very much as in the Hooded Seal. It begins to be obvious when the young male is about two years old and reaches its full size by about eight years. It is not very obvious in the non-breeding season, but when excited by the need to preserve territory during the breeding season it may become blown up, partly by air and partly by muscular action and by blood pressure. The harsh roar of the male comes from the mouth, the proboscis acting as a resonator. The function appears to be slightly different in the Northern Elephant Seal where the snout is larger. When roaring the snout hangs down inside the mouth with the nostrils directed towards the pharynx. The nasal snorts are thus directed down the throat which acts as a resonating chamber.

6

Some characteristics of Pinnipedia

The external shape of a seal or sea lion is unmistakably adapted for an aquatic life[8,9]. The streamlining of the body has already been mentioned, with its elimination of unnecessary protuberances and the development of flippers. The fore-flippers of an otariid are broad, oar-like structures with naked black palms and the nails reduced to small nodules. The strong first digit is further strengthened by fibrous tissue along the leading edge and more of this tissue fills in the spaces between the digits. Cartilaginous extensions beyond the tips of the digits make the flipper larger. Those extensions on the hind flipper protrude beyond the normal edge of the flipper and those of the middle three digits can be folded back so that their long nails can be used for scratching. The powerful front flippers are used as oars when swimming and are the main means of propulsion. The hind flippers are held soles together and used as a rudder. On land the front flippers are used to support the body and they extend sideways with a right-angle bend at the wrist. The hind flippers can be brought forwards with their soles flat on the ground and a walking or galloping movement can be achieved. Progression is by no means slothful and a sea lion can easily walk quickly up a ladder balancing a ball on its nose.

The phocid fore-flipper is covered with fur on both surfaces and usually has well developed claws. There are usually no cartilaginous extensions and except in the more specialized members the digits are all of approximately the same length. The Ross Seal for example has a specialized fore flipper more like that of an otariid with its elongated first digit and reduced claws. The hind flipper has the two outer digits longest, fur on both sides, and the digits connected by expansile skin. Swimming power comes from the hind end of the body, the strokes of the hind flippers being assisted by lateral movements of the body. The fore flippers are held close against the sides of the body except when changing direction or when some fine adjustment of direction is needed. As the hind flippers cannot be brought forward under the body they can take no part in terrestrial locomotion and either trail along behind or are lifted clear of the ground. Movement over land is achieved by alternately taking the body weight on the sternum and on the pelvis, using a caterpillar hitching movement. Grey Seals can use the strong haulage grip of the terminal phalanges of the fore flippers to assist them over rocky or difficult ground. It is probable that other members of the Phocinae have a similar grip.

Although we describe pinnipeds as marine mammals they differ from cetaceans in that they can live reasonably happily for many years without being in the sea at all. Most seals spend a considerable part of each day on land, usually fast asleep, but again they do not have to come ashore and can survive, and sleep, in the sea for as long as is necessary. Grey Seals and Common Seals can dive for over 20 minutes if forced to but usually they seldom dive for longer than a few minutes at a time[95]. Weddell Seals probably stay submerged for the longest periods of all pinnipeds, sometimes well over 60 minutes. Young seals are not such good divers as adults, though newborn Common Seal pups can tolerate dives lasting for several minutes. Both seals and sea lions can dive to considerable depths and return quickly to the surface. There are reports of quite young Grey Seals reaching 70 fathoms, but the record for diving depth is held by the Weddell Seal. Free swimming animals at an Antarctic breathing hole are fitted with a package of electronic recording instruments that indicate that they are able to descend to over 300 fathoms while on feeding expeditions[109].

SKULL AND SKELETON

The pinniped skull and skeleton are less modified than those of cetaceans and sirenians[4]. The skull, although character-

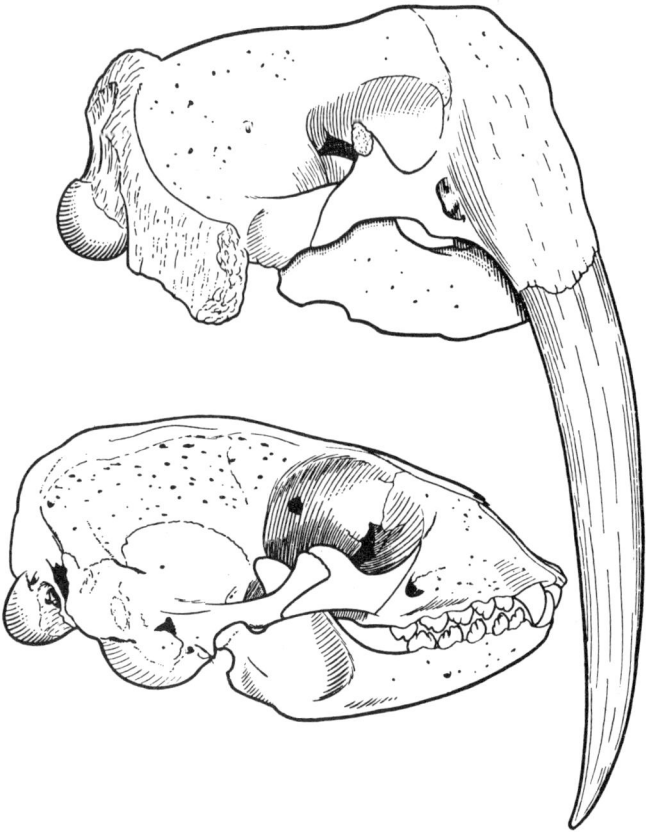

Fig. 7. Skulls of walrus (top) and Common Seal (below)

istically different from genus to genus, has its component parts more easily recognizable than in a cetacean for example. A basic dog-like shape is evident but the cranium is particularly large, the interorbital region long and parallel-sided, the snout short and the orbits large. The lacrimal bone is absent in phocids. There is no nasolacrimal duct and there are no cranial air sinuses.

Skulls of Otariidae and Odobenidae are distinguished[9,98] by their small, flattened tympanic bullae, the larger mastoid processes and the presence of an alisphenoid canal. Phocid skulls have inflated tympanic bullae, smaller mastoid processes and no alisphenoid canals (Fig. 7). Its truncated anterior end makes a walrus skull quite unmistakable. The entire snout region is given up to housing the roots of the enormous tusks so that the maxillae are expanded and modified and the nasal opening is very small. There are no post-orbital processes, no sagittal crest, and the entire skull is heavily ossified. Otariid skulls have postorbital processes, well developed sagittal crests and a deep transverse groove in the first two upper incisors on each side of the jaw.

Members of the two phocid subfamilies may be distinguished by various characters of skull and skeleton[105]. Some of these may be mentioned. The Phocinae have an elongated foramen lacerum posterius between the bulla and basioccipital, and the basioccipital-basisphenoid area is flat. The spine on the scapula is well formed, and the metacarpals of digits 1 and 2 are nearly the same size. The Monachinae have the bulla applied to the basioccipital and the foramen lacerum posterius is small. The basisphenoid area is concave. The scapular spine is reduced, and the first metacarpal is longer and stronger than the others.

The vertebral column reflects in its processes the different movements of otariid and phocid. That of the walrus is in most respects intermediate. An otariid has the main muscular power at the front end of the body and thus the neural spines of the thoracic vertebrae are correspondingly long. The emphasis in the phocid spine is at the posterior end and the transverse processes of the lumbar vertebrae are well developed, while the loosely fitting zygapophyses allow considerable range of movement. The mobility of the spine is seen at its greatest extent in the Southern Elephant Seal which can bend backwards so that the top of its head can touch its tail.

The sternum is composed of eight or nine pieces. The manubrium has a long bony extension in the Otariidae but it is cartilaginous in the phocids and walrus. There is no clavicle. The otariid and walrus scapulae have well developed spines towards the posterior third of the blade and the otariid has in addition a bony ridge anterior to the spine. The phocid scapula has a much smaller spine centrally placed. The general pattern of the fore limb skeleton is similar in all pinnipeds (Fig. 2). The humerus, radius and ulna are short and the latter two bones are flattened, the ulna at its proximal end and the radius at its distal end. Although short these bones are strong and give attachment to many muscles.

The carpal elements are crowded towards the ulnar side in phocids as a result of the position in which the flipper is held. The flippers of the less specialized northern phocids have good articulations between the phalangeal bones and can bend the terminal phalanx to get a strong haulage grip. No one digit is conspicuously longer than the others and they all bear strong claws. The more specialized flippers of the Antarctic phocids have flatter bones with less movement between them, and the bones of the first digit are longer and stronger. The flattened endings of the otariid terminal phalanges are where the cartilaginous extensions are attached but show only slight indications of the reduced claws.

The pelvis is composed of the normal three elements but has the ischium and pubis elongated and the ilium shortened. The latter is twisted in Phocinae so that the lateral border faces more posteriorly giving a greater area of attachment on the now anterior surface to one of the muscles concerned in swimming movements. There is no symphysis pubis. The femur is short and flattened, the tibia and fibula are fused at their proximal ends and bound together by ligaments at their distal ends. The phocid astragalus has an elongated process so that it and the calcaneum are nearly the same length. A strong tendon running over the prolongation of the astragalus prevents the forward movement of the foot that is characteristic of the other two families. The bones of the first digit are particularly strong in all seals and as in the fore flipper the bones of the otariid hind flipper are flatter. An os penis or baculum is present in all seals and in the larger animals may grow to a considerable size—as long as 70 cm in a walrus. The length of the baculum has been used to age many types of seal. The female counterpart, the os clitoris, is present in many seals but is small.

TEETH

The teeth[9] of all members of the Otariidae are of the same general form, showing only minor although sometimes characteristic variations in size or cusping. The dental formula is $i\frac{2}{3}$, $c\frac{1}{1}$, *pc$\frac{5 \text{ or } 6}{5}$; the most characteristic feature, the transverse groove on each of the first two upper incisors has already been mentioned. The milk dentition is poorly developed. Small deciduous incisors and canines are present but only the second, third and fourth postcanines are preceded by milk teeth. These are very small pin-like teeth, seldom larger than 8 mm in even the largest animals and all being shed by the time the seal is 6 months old.

The Phocinae have incisors $\frac{3}{2}$, the Monachinae $\frac{2}{2}$. Exceptions[105] to both subfamilies are Cystophora and Mirounga with $\frac{2}{1}$. The postcanines are normally $\frac{5}{5}$. Although some phocids, such as Halichoerus and Mirounga, have relatively simple cheek teeth, there is much more variation in the pattern of the post-canines than in the Otariidae. The degree of cusping ranges from the simple rounded cusps of Phoca to the delicately pointed ones of Pusa and the long, strong

*These teeth are little differentiated from one another in shape and usually referred to as postcanines or cheek teeth.

points of *Hydrurga*; the characteristic recurved cusps of *Lobodon* are the most complicated (Fig. 4). The Monk Seals have broad, heavy cheek teeth; those of the Bearded Seal quickly wear flat and may drop out; those of the Ross Seal are also small and weak. The milk teeth are usually either resorbed before birth or shed very shortly after birth. They may sometimes be seen as small bony nodules in the gum tissue and have been known to persist in this state for as long as three years. Work on Crabeater, Weddell and Elephant Seals has shown that the developing milk teeth are detectable by X-rays about 6 weeks after implantation of the blastocyst and reach their maximum development at about 3 months of foetal life. The permanent dentition is usually fully erupted by the time the pup is a month old.

The walrus undoubtedly has the most modified teeth of all pinnipeds[87,116]. The characteristic long tusks are the upper canines (Fig. 7). They are present in both sexes but are a little more slender in females. Tusks of between 70 and 90 cm long are quite common and a particularly large one may reach a length of 1·0 m with a weight of over 5 kg. They erupt when a walrus is about four months old and are nearly a foot long after 5 years. The pulp cavity remains open and the tusk continues to grow throughout life. The central core of granular dentine is characteristic of walrus ivory and the nature of carvings may often be identified in this way. Behind the tusks in the upper jaw there are four flattish teeth on each side. It has been established by reference to the milk teeth that these are the third incisor and three post-canines. The four similar flat teeth on each side of the lower jaw are the canine and three post-canines. The usual number of milk teeth are produced and are shed shortly after birth but not all of them are succeeded by permanent teeth. There are, for instance, no permanent incisors in the lower jaw. Sometimes a small permanent second upper incisor erupts and also an extra post-canine.

The age[110] of many seals has been estimated reasonably

accurately by counting the number of rings in the roots of the canines, rather like the annual rings in the trunk of a tree. There is of course no further growth of the enamel crown after the tooth has erupted but there is deposition of dentine on the inner surface of the pulp cavity, in concentric layers, and it is these that can be counted. In the Southern Elephant Seal[111] in particular the dense dentine layers are laid down during breeding, moulting and pregnancy and are separated by lighter layers so that a series of these rings represents a year in the life of the seal. There is some connection between the deposition of dense dentine and the state of activity of the gonads but many hormones other than gonadal stimulate the production of dentine and thus obscure the picture. Annual rings can sometimes be seen in the cement layers on the outside of the root, and annual, light coloured bands on claws have been used as age indicators but not very successfully as the claws get worn away.

FEEDING HABITS

Most seals are fairly catholic in their feeding habits and although fish and cephalopods are the most usual foods, krill and other crustaceans, molluscs and holothurians are also taken[9,15]. The type of fish varies of course with the part of the world the seal lives in, but it is naturally the most commonly occurring fish of the area that are eaten. Where these are also commercially valuable the desires of seal and man come into conflict and a difficult and sometimes insoluble situation develops. Fish of moderate size are swallowed whole, head first so that the mouth is not scratched by the spiny fins; large fish are less often caught and are then torn in pieces. Exact determination of the food eaten depends on examination of the stomach contents. This is often difficult because seals catch their food while at sea, digestion is rapid and so the stomachs of animals killed while on land are nearly always empty; seals killed at sea usually sink and are difficult to retrieve. Pups after weaning may start by catching small pelagic crustaceans and small fish before proceeding to the adult diet. The Crabeater feeds almost entirely on krill (p. 57) and its curious cheek teeth are adapted for this purpose. Leopard Seals, although eating mostly fish and squid, may sometimes attack the pups of other seals and they will also catch penguins under water. These are brought to the surface and shaken so hard that the skins, turned inside out, are sometimes found on the ice. Associated with swallowing this bulky food the trachea is found to be supported by cartilage on its ventral side only. The soft tissue on the dorsal side allows for compression of the tracheal lumen without damage.

The walrus has interesting though puzzling feeding habits. Food consists almost entirely of bivalve molluscs and the walrus searches for these on the shallow, gravelly sea bottom by stirring it up with its tusks and then using the mobile, sensitive lips and whiskers to sort the food. Examination of stomach contents has shown that in spite of its diet the walrus only very seldom swallows any pieces of shell. The fleshy siphons and feet of the molluscs are swallowed whole and it seems very likely that they are sucked out of their shells. Mussel shells that appear to have been treated in this way are often found round walrus breathing holes. This does not explain, however, how the cheek teeth get worn so flat. The full stomach of an adult walrus has been recorded as weighing 50 kg and must have contained the remains of nearly 600 molluscs. Walruses occasionally eat pups of other seals but usually only when other food is scarce. Bearded Seals also eat molluscs and show similarities to walruses in that they have a large array of whiskers, seldom have remains of shells in their stomachs, and also get very worn cheek teeth. It may be that they also obtain much of their food by sucking.

The stomachs of many seals have been found to contain stones, sometimes a large number of small stones, sometimes only a few but larger stones, up to the size of a tennis ball. They appear to be taken in deliberately but to what purpose has never yet been satisfactorily determined. Explanations have ranged from the stones being necessary to grind up stomach parasites or food; to weight the animal when it is thin from fasting, or when it is fat and buoyant; or to provide bulk for the stomach during periods of fasting. It is known that seals can survive for many months without eating and they almost certainly all fast during lactation. It is interesting that crocodiles also swallow stones, their total weight giving an indication of the age of the animal; this does not seem to apply to seals as yearlings have been found to contain surprisingly large stones while adults may lack them altogether.

Seals are usually infested with numerous parasites[3] of several kinds. Nematodes, acanthocephalans, trematodes and cestodes are found in the gut and nematodes also occur in the heart, lungs and blood vessels. Mites are frequently found in the nasal cavity and ticks are attached to the skin. Only when they occur in enormous numbers in the adult host do the parasites cause appreciable damage. Where the problem has been studied, for instance in the Pribilof Fur Seal, it has been shown that nematode infestation is one of the main causes of death in young pups. Seal pups have to contend not only with parasites but with overcrowding and possible trampling to death by large bulls, starvation, abandonment by the cow, getting washed away by heavy seas, and also bacterial infections. It has been estimated that over half the pups born in any one year do not survive for a year. The normal bacterial flora of seals has been little studied but it is known that they are susceptible to lung infections giving rise to a form of bronchopneumonia, perhaps secondary to parasitic infestation. The lymphatic nodes of seals are strikingly developed. Other enemies, such as Killer Whales, sharks, and of course man, attack seals of all ages. In spite of this seals have been recorded as living to a reasonable age. Marked animals on the Pribilof Islands have been seen after 21 years and from counting the tooth rings it has been estimated that Grey Seals in the wild have lived up to 46 years. There are many records of seals living in captivity up to 20 years and there is a well known Grey Seal that lived in a Swedish zoo for 41 years.

SKIN, FUR AND BLUBBER

The skin of seals has an unusual multiplicity of functions and adaptations[13,113]. On the surface are the hairs, sometimes characteristically coloured and sometimes so dense that they constitute a commercially valuable fur, and below is the fatty blubber which in the large Elephant Seal is also used commercially. The hairs grow in groups, each consisting of a single stiff flattened guard hair with a variable number of finer underfur hairs posterior to it (Fig. 5). The hairs in each group grow from separate follicles but emerge to the surface through a single pilary canal. The underfur hairs trap small air bubbles which probably help in keeping the skin dry and the harsher guard hairs protect the body from abrasion. Fur seals may have about nineteen underfur follicles and while the number of follicles remains unchanged, at each moult some of the hairs remain fast in the pilary canal so that the number of hairs in each group increases during life up to nearly seventy. This of course increases the thickness and value of the pelt and strangely the hairs remain firm even when the skin is dressed. Phocids and sea lions have only about 2–5 underfur hairs in each group. Resting hair follicles have been found to have a thickened, partly keratinized collar gripping the hair above the club and preventing water from entering the follicle.

In the Common Seal, and probably in other phocids too, the epidermis is thick and well pigmented and the stratum granulosum is missing. The cells of the outer layer, the stratum corneum, are peculiar in being nucleated like those of mucous membranes such as the oesophageal lining. This would mean a softer and more permanent outer layer to the skin, that is much less likely to be waterlogged and flake off than a layer of dead horny cells. The waterproof film that protects the hair and body of seals is secreted by the many large sebaceous glands that open into each pilary canal, and one coiled apocrine sweat gland also opens into each canal. The almost solid non-fatty secretion of these glands may possibly be a waste product and it may be responsible for the curious characteristic smell of seals. There is increase in the activity of the glands when breeding and moulting. The upper layer of the dermis is notable for being very vascular, the dilated venules forming sinuses that may have some function in heat regulation and as a blood reservoir. The lower reticular layer of the dermis is a fibrous mesh with the pilary canals in the upper portion and its lower layers merging with the blubber.

The skins of fur seals and sea lions are slightly different. The epidermis is thinner, the corneal cells appear to be of the normal non-nucleated type and there is only a single pair of sebaceous glands to each pilary canal. The method of moulting in these animals, too, appears to be quite normal.

The moult of phocids is of a more unusual nature and may even be said to be spectacular in the Elephant Seal and Laysan Monk Seal where it has been especially noticed. An increase in the vascularity of the skin and in the functioning of the sweat glands is followed by the development of new hairs. The upper layer of the skin becomes 'normal' by the appearance of a stratum granulosum and cornified cells which are then shed in patches, sometimes as much as a foot square. These tattered pieces of skin carry with them the old hairs, the roots protruding on one side and the tips on the other. The life of the Southern Elephant Seal has been studied in some detail: these seals remain on land without feeding for about a month while they are moulting, perhaps some indication that this method of moulting seriously upsets their metabolism.

Southern Elephant Seals, because of their large size and gregarious habits during part of the year, have been the obvious choice for hunting for their blubber, the oil from which is used together with vegetable oils in the manufacture of good edible fats. The blubber, which may be, up to 15 cm thick, is pulled off in one piece from each seal after cuts have been made round the head, fore flippers and hind end, the skinning of one seal taking perhaps 3 or 4 minutes. The South African and Pribilof Fur Seals are the otaries most usually taken for their fur and as with the Elephant Seal it is the polygamous nature of their breeding habits that allows the surplus bulls to be taken without detriment to the herd. Fur seal skins have the blubber removed and over a hundred different processes then take place before the skin is dressed, supple and finished. As the roots of the guard hairs are deeper than those of the under-fur hairs they can be destroyed by scraping the under side of the skin, when the guard hairs fall out. The underfur hairs are straightened and dyed. The very young white coated pups of the Harp Seal are taken for their thick natal fur coat and the patterned coats of the young Hooded Seal and adult Ringed Seal are also used. The former is known as a 'blueback' because of the steely blue dorsal surface sharply demarcated from the creamy ventral surface, resulting in a very characteristic and beautiful fur coat.

TEMPERATURE REGULATION

Mammals that spend a large part of their lives in water and some in Arctic and Antarctic water, must be able to maintain their body temperature efficiently[13,96,101]. The high metabolic rate of seals and the layer of blubber round their bodies helps to do this and the thick underfur of fur seals keeps them adequately warm. The average internal body temperature is about 36·5°–37·5°C (97·7°–99·5°F) but there is much variation. Although fur seals can keep warm, they cannot so easily cool themselves and they may die from heat exhaustion if their body temperature rises much above 41°C. It is a characteristic sight in a rookery of fur seals to see the animals lazily fanning themselves with their outstretched hind flippers. The passage of air over the thin black flippers, which are well supplied both with sweat glands that appear to have a liquid secretion and with a good vascular supply, is the fur seal's chief method of cooling.

The thin coat of phocids is of no help in keeping them warm but they have evolved a different method that is more efficient as it can be more precisely regulated. As the ambient temperature decreases so the arterioles of the skin contract and the skin cools down to a temperature about one degree warmer than the water, just sufficient to prevent it freezing. This prevents heat from leaving the body and there is thus a steep gradient between the skin with its low temperature and about 3·8 cm deep in the body where the temperature is practically constant. This insulation of the centre of the animal from its environment means that the seal does not have to increase its metabolism in order to keep warm. When necessary, cooling of the body can be quickly achieved by relaxing the arterioles and warming up the skin.

VISCERAL ANATOMY

The pinniped alimentary canal is uncomplicated, the stomach a simple enlargement, the caecum absent or hardly distinct and the intestine long. Although sufficient measurements of the length of the small intestine of enough species of seal have not been taken enough are known to make its great length remarkable. A man has a small intestine about 7 m long, a Southern Sea Lion of nose to tail length 1·7 m has a small intestine 18 m long and in a 5 m Elephant Seal it has a length of 130 m[9]. There is much individual variation in the lengths but there is some indication that the intestine of a carnivorous seal such as the Leopard may be shorter. The liver is deeply divided into about six long pointed lobes and a gall bladder is present. Livers of some seals, particularly of Bearded Seals and of large Ringed Seals and walruses, are avoided by Eskimoes and even by their dogs as the very high content of vitamin A makes them unpleasant to eat and even poisonous. Small quantities may be eaten without ill effect and dogs will eat a frozen liver.

The seal kidney[8,9] is lobulated and looks like a com-

5

pressed, flattened bunch of grapes (Fig. 5). Each of these 'grapes' or renules, of which there may be many hundred in each kidney, are self-contained units each a miniature kidney with its own blood supply, papilla, calyx and excretory duct joining with those of other renules to form the ureter. The extent to which the outer fibrous capsule of the entire organ follows the lobulations differs considerably as does the degree of separation of each renule from its neighbour. It is not possible to separate the renules in the Otariidae and the fibrous capsule remains on the outside of the kidney. With increasing specialization the fibrous coat dips down between the renules, separating groups of them as in *P. vitulina* and eventually isolating each renule as in *O. rossi*. The possible significance of the lobulation is discussed on p. 77. It is possible that the renules display intermittency of activity. Urinary concentrating mechanisms[13,97] are well developed in seals but diving reduces the glomerular filtration rate. It is said that seals obtain most of their water for metabolic purposes from their food and there is a marked postprandial diuresis after taking food or water[13].

Except in male Elephant Seals and Hooded Seals with their marked probosces (Fig. 6), the nostrils are in the normal position at the end of the snout; only in the Monachinae have they moved to a more horizontal position. The normal, relaxed condition of the nostrils is closed[100]; entry of water when the seal is submerged is prevented by pressure of the moustachial pads against the nasal septum and may well be made more effective by the pressure of the water. In forced respiration the nostrils can be dilated widely to produce a snorting noise; seals can also sneeze violently and snore loudly. The trachea in phocids and walruses divides into two very short bronchi which immediately enter the substance of the lung, but in otariids the trachea divides at the level of the first rib and the long bronchi extend close together and parallel into the thorax. The lungs[6,13] are remarkably symmetrical in construction and in arrangement of bronchial tree and vessels. They often show a lobulated appearance on surface examination and there are plentiful subpleural vessels. The terminal airways are supported right up to the alveoli with muscle (phocids) and cartilage (otaries, walrus), as in cetaceans[88]. Analyses of expired air after dives have been made by Scholander[139]. The diaphragm is more obliquely placed than in terrestrial mammals and the more dorsal position of the lungs may be useful when buoyancy is needed. The curious pharyngeal pouches of the walrus are most probably also used for this purpose. These pouches are formed from the expanded, very elastic lateral walls of the pharynx and they extend backwards between the muscles of the neck as far as the scapula or even to the posterior end of the thoracic cavity. They can be inflated with air from the lungs, which is then prevented from escaping by muscular constrictors. Pouches have not been found in young walruses, nor yet in every adult examined. The breathing rhythm of pinnipeds is irregular, as might perhaps be expected from their way of life. When asleep Common Seals take fifteen to eighteen breaths a minute but when awake there are often long respiratory pauses, occasionally for as long as 10 minutes, followed by numerous rapid breaths. Seals often exhale under water during a dive and almost always exhale when they break the surface after a dive[13,93].

Modifications of the pinniped vascular system[6,13,95] are chiefly confined to the veins (Fig. 5), although not all the features displayed are known to be necessarily related to an aquatic life. Venous drainage of the cranium and brain is mainly by the hypocondylar veins leading into the extradural intravertebral vein (Fig. 8). The internal jugular system is reduced and only drains extracranial tissues. The extradural vein in phocids is a large thin-walled vessel lying dorsal to the spinal cord and its importance is indicated by the numerous connections it has with other parts of the venous system. Anteriorly it receives vessels from a large venous plexus in the dorsal musculature, from segmental veins in the thoracic region and from the large azygos veins. There are large communications with the renal and pelvic plexuses and from segmental veins in the lumbar and sacral

Fig. 8. Venous pattern and caval sphincter in seal
Top: diagram of the venous pattern in a Common Seal
Below: diagram of the caval sphincter and pericardial venous network in a Common Seal

regions. It has been shown by injection of radio-opaque materials that blood flow in the extradural vein is very free and that blood passes from the heart into it within seconds. Injection into the vein provides an easy and safe method of administering drugs or anaesthetics.

In the kidney the fine veins from each renule drain into interlobular veins which come to the surface to drain into the striking stellate plexus of veins that lies on the front and back of the organ in the grooves between the renules (Fig. 5). Three main veins pass from the stellate plexus to drain into the posterior vena cava; there are also numerous communications to lumbar plexuses as well as the important connections with the extradural vein mentioned above. The posterior vena cava is duplicated in seals, it is thin-walled and relative to the size of the animal is very large. (It is not surprising perhaps that the blood volume relative to the weight of the body is $1\frac{1}{2}$ to 2 times that of other mammals including man.) The limbs of the posterior vena cava receive blood from the posterior end of the body, from the plexuses draining the flippers and pelvis, from the stellate renal plexus, and from the extradural vein. The two limbs join anterior to the kidneys to form a single vessel which traverses the liver to enter the so-called hepatic sinus (Figs. 5 and 8). This is a dilatation of the vena cava cranial to the liver but caudal to the diaphragm. The sinus receives the hepatic veins which are often very dilated at their point of entry and which may have muscle in their walls. An hepatic sinus of this type is not found except in seals and its large size is remarkable. It can hold over a litre of blood in an adult Common Seal. Associated with the hepatic sinus and also found only in seals in such a developed state is the caval sphincter[6,94,95]. This is a funnel shaped band of striated muscle, 5 cm long in the Common Seal, which surrounds the posterior vena cava just anterior to the diaphragm to which it is attached by connective tissue and some muscle fibres (Fig. 8). It is supplied by the right phrenic nerve but it does not necessarily contract when the diaphragm does. Experimental work[6,94,95] suggests that it contracts during diving and that it controls the venous return to the heart in association with the bradycardia (see later) that develops when a seal submerges.

Cranial to the sphincter the vena cava receives veins from a pericardial plexus almost retial in nature (p. 71) which projects all round the base of the pericardium and which is capable of considerable enlargement. It may act as a spacefiller, or the brown fat in its construction may be thermoregulatory[83]. The paired azygos veins, which are large in seals, are formed from lateral tributaries of the extradural vein with contributions from the anterior part of the stellate renal plexus. The right azygos becomes considerably larger in the thorax and drains practically all the blood from the intercostal veins of both sides into the anterior vena cava. Communications between the intercostal veins and the extradural vein link the latter with the azygos system. The principal observations just described were made on phocids, particularly the Common Seal. The veins in otariids and walruses are less modified. Typically mammalian are the paired lateral extradural veins, external jugular and single renal vein. There are no stellate or pericardial plexuses and the hepatic sinus develops only in the adult[108].

DIVING

A first requisite for an animal that spends a considerable time below the surface is to keep the water out of its respiratory system. This a seal does by an efficient closing of its nostrils. The arrangement of the nasal cartilage is such that pressure on it by the moustachial pad, and of course by water pressure as well, efficiently seals the nostrils against the entry of water. They are opened by muscular contraction which lifts the moustachial pad. Muscular arrangements within the larynx are directed more towards withstanding pressure than the production of sound. Breathing out on diving reduces the amount of air in the lungs so that the remainder can be kept in the rigid, less absorptive parts, is less subject to pressure and the seal is unlikely to suffer from 'bends' (p. 69). The immediate result of cessation of respiration and submersion is the remarkable slowing down of the heart rate. There is normally considerable variation in the heart rate[6,13,95], that of pups being about 90–180 beats a minute while in adults it is 55–120 beats a minute, but immediately on diving it slows to between about 4–15 beats a minute. This diving bradycardia is also shown by muskrats, coypus and beavers and to a much lesser extent by cetaceans (p. 70). Young seal pups even during their first week of life can remain under water for 8 minutes, while older seals can dive for at least half an hour if necessary, though it seems most likely that 5–10 minutes is the normal time that is spent under water. On return to the surface after a long dive there is a recovery tachycardia that lasts for up to 10 minutes before the heart returns to its normal rate.

Much experimental work on diving has been done on Common Seals and other forms[6,13,93]. Animals have been secured to boards and immersed in shallow tanks, or in deeper water under pressure and their heart rates recorded. It has been seen that after the initial bradycardia the heart rate increases very slowly until the animal is brought to the surface again. Bradycardia develops more rapidly, is slower, and lasts longer in the older seals. It has been discovered experimentally that the cutting of both vagus nerves after a seal has submerged results in an immediate rise in the heart rate. Dissection of the vagus has shown that there is a close relationship between it and the sympathetic trunk, both of which innervate the heart, and that there are two small ganglia, apparently unique to seals, on the sympathetic trunk which have connections with the vagus and phrenic nerves, a connection that may be significant as the right phrenic nerve innervates the caval sphincter.

Most terrestrial mammals, man included, can only remain submerged about 2–3 minutes without breathing, reaction to increased carbon dioxide in the blood and brain damage from lack of oxygen occurring quite quickly. Seals then, in order to stay down for longer periods, must conserve the oxygen in the blood and must keep the brain supplied. To keep the blood to the essential organs the peripheral blood vessels are constricted and much of the muscular activity is anaerobic. Anyone who has cut up a seal will appreciate the large amount of blood, three-quarters as much again as in a man of similar weight. As well as the oxygen carried in the blood, more is stored in the myoglobin of the muscles. This extra amount of oxygen together with its slow consumption and the lower degree of sensitivity to carbon dioxide is sufficient for diving. It is probable that the venous blood returning to the heart can be dammed back in the hepatic sinus by the contraction of the caval sphincter, small amounts of blood being let through with consequent increase in the heart rate until so much oxygen has been used up that the animal has to surface. See also p. 69 for a discussion on diving by cetaceans.

See also p. 69

BRAIN

Little detailed investigation of the pinniped brain has been made apart from descriptions of the general configuration, the fissure arrangement in the cerebral cortex in different species and the appearances of the cerebellum[18,35]. Brain weight in adults varies from about 250 g in *Phoca* to 380 g in *Zalophus* and up to 1,000 g in *Odobenus*. The bony tentorium between the cerebrum and the cerebellum is well developed and the brain is foreshortened, more spherical and more convoluted[13,14] than that of a terrestrial carnivore. The position of the excito-motor cortex is known and the seal's body is represented on it approximately upside down. Its histological characteristics do not differ markedly from those of terrestrial mammals. The auditory and trigeminal sensory areas are large and obviously important. The entire trigeminal nuclear complex reaches its greatest size among carnivores in *Phoca*. The superficial olfactory apparatus varies in complexity, being better developed in otariids than phocids, but in none is it as well developed as in macrosmatic carnivores. The cerebellum is large compared with that in other carnivores as also is the pons. The large size is produced by the well developed paraflocculus and the relatively enlarged flocculonodular lobe. The lobus simplex and ansiform lobule are small, thus differing from cetaceans in which the lobulus simplex is large.

Discussion of the characteristics of the cetacean brain that might be related to a marine existence will be found on p. 86. Some similar features are also present in the pinniped brain but it seems certain that seals have not evolved such a highly organized central nervous system as is possessed by cetaceans. Although they can be taught simple tricks (sea lions can be trained more easily than seals mainly because they are more mobile on land) the behaviour of pinnipeds generally is little if any more advanced than their terrestrial relatives.

SENSES

Of the senses, sight and hearing are the most developed. In order to appreciate as much light as possible under water and also to perceive their fast moving prey, the eyeballs are very large. In the smaller seals, the Ringed Seal, for example, the eyes are out of proportion with the small skull and in order to accommodate them in the head at all the inter-orbital part of the skull has to be reduced to such thinness that it is almost transparent. Tears are apt to run from the seal's large, appealing circular eyes down its face, inspiring sympathy, when in fact the wateriness occurs only because they lack a naso-lacrimal duct. A protective oil is secreted over the cornea. The eyes are adapted for seeing clearly both in water and on land. When under water the pupil is expanded into a wide circle so as to let in as much light as possible. The function of the cornea is lost, as it has the same refractive index as the water, so that the lens is thickened until it is almost spherical to compensate for this. In air the pupil is contracted to a slit that is vertical in most seals. Excessive accommodation for the change from water to air is avoided by having a high degree of corneal astigmatism. The combination of the slit pupil lying parallel to the astigmatic axis will focus a point as a point on the retina and will thus eliminate the astigmatism of the system. The retina is backed by a tapetum.

The external ear is reduced to a small tightly furled pinna in the Otariidae and even this is missing in the walrus and Phocidae. Cartilages support the pinna when it is present and are curled round the external auditory meatus when it is not. Most northern phocids have the cartilages extending the entire length of the external meatus, but Antarctic phocids have cartilage only at the inner end of the passage, the rest being unsupported and very narrow, the external opening being only big enough to admit a pin. The ear muscles are reduced and it is improbable that they could open or close the meatus, closing most probably being achieved by water pressure. The structure of the middle and inner ear conforms in general to the mammalian pattern. Hearing is good in air, but better and very directional underwater. Engorgement of middle ear cavernous tissue on diving equalizes pressure and underwater hearing may be through the bones of the skull as well as the ossicles[119]. Underwater sounds have recently been recorded from both phocids and otariids[13]. Rather faint impulses have been detected when the animals were close to the hydrophone and it has been suggested that these are probably used in the last stages of catching the fish and that other louder sounds may be made by seals in the wild. Seals that are blind in one or both eyes are not infrequently found and it has been interesting to speculate how they have remained so well fed. If, as seems probable, they find their food by echolocation then whole or partial blindness is obviously no serious handicap.

Little is known about the sense of smell but the small olfactory lobes of the brain and the reduced ethmoturbinals do not suggest that it is very acute. It is probable though that the final stages in locating a pup on a crowded beach are olfactory and the odour of the sweat glands during the breeding season is presumably appreciated. Taste has not really been investigated but as the animals swallow their food whole it might be expected that there would not be any great development of taste buds though they are definitely present. Seals seem to vary a good deal in their awareness of touch: some, like the Monk Seals, rarely touch each other, while Elephant Seals lie close together with their bodies in contact. The moustachial whiskers, particularly in those animals where they are well developed, are used for examining food and strange surfaces and their abundant nerve supply indicates their sensitiveness.

In general, and as might be expected, most seals of the northern hemisphere produce their pups in the northern spring and summer from about February to July and all seals of the southern hemisphere pup from September to January[2]. This division breaks down in some instances in an interesting way. Both Northern and Southern Elephant Seals[81,112] pup in the latter half of the year in spite of *M. angustirostris* living north of the Equator. The Mediterranean and West Indian Monk Seals pup from September onwards as do their relatives the Weddell and Crabeater Seals, but it is strange that the Laysan Monk Seal has a typical northern hemisphere pupping time. The British population of Grey Seals on the other hand pup very late in the year for a northern animal. Californian Sea Lions off California pup in midsummer but those on the Galapagos Islands just south of the Equator have changed their pupping time to October until December. Similarly the Guadalupe Fur Seal pups in June, but the Galapagos and Juan Fernandez Fur Seals have changed to the southern hemisphere time of December.

All male otariids, and of phocids male Elephant Seals and Grey Seals, establish territories and collect harems of females at breeding time. The number of females in each harem varies; Steller's Sea Lions have 10–20, Pribilof Fur Seals about 50, southern Elephant Seals 20–40 although sometimes as many as 100, but most others have about a dozen or less[112]. The general pattern of harem behaviour as far as it is known is much the same for all these animals, with some variation in details. It has been particularly studied in the southern Elephant Seal and the Pribilof Fur Seal because of their commercial importance. The harem bulls come ashore first. These are the large powerful bulls capable of holding a territory and defending it. They may not achieve this status until they are nearly 12 years old although they are sexually mature at about 4–6 years old. The cows come ashore about a fortnight after the bulls and are quickly gathered into harems. Those bulls in the more favourable positions on the shore are able to waylay more females. For the next two months the bulls are fully occupied mating, challenging and fighting and do not return to the sea to feed until after the breeding season is over. The mature bulls that have not yet achieved harem owner-ship or territorial status remain separate but not too far from the edges of the harems where they endeavour to obtain females and occasionally to challenge the harem bull. Amongst Elephant Seals the challenger makes his intentions clear by roaring and this alone may sometimes be successful although usually the harem bull roars back. Should an exchange of roaring and threatening have no effect then a fight usually develops. This natural segregation of the bachelors makes the work of the commercial sealer much easier.

The pups are born about a week after the cows come on land. Birth is rapid, the pup usually appears head first and the umbilical cord is broken by a swift movement of the mother's hindquarters. All fur seal pups are born with black, rather woolly coats that are shed after about 2 months for a coat more like that of the parents. Most sea lions also have a thicker coat when pups. The length of the lactation period varies but in otariids is about 4–6 months. The Pribilof Fur Seal cow remains with her pup for about a week and goes to sea to feed returning one day a week to suckle her pup. The pups gather in groups known as 'pods' while the cows are away and spend much time sleeping and

playing. The Elephant Seal cows on the other hand feed
their pups for a month and remain with them without going
to sea for food[112]. Most pups are able to swim shortly after
birth, but the great majority wait for about a month before
venturing into the sea. There is little parental care; the bulls
in particular are quite indifferent and not infrequently
squash pups by rolling on them. Mating in otariids takes
place about a week after the birth of the pup: in the Elephant
Seal it occurs after 18 days and afterwards the harem system
begins to break up.

Apart from those animals already mentioned the rest of
the Phocidae are monogamous as far as is known, though
evidence of promiscuity is not lacking for some forms.
Certainly some of them, such as Harp and Hooded Seals,
form family groups of male, female and pup on the ice at
breeding time. Ringed Seal cows may excavate lairs under
the snow to shelter their pups. Pups of *Pusa*, *Pagophilus*,
Histriophoca and also *Halichoerus* are covered in thick
yellowish white fur at birth; it is shed after about three
weeks. *Monachus* pups have a black woolly coat, and
Erignathus and the Antarctic seals a grey woolly coat.
Phoca pups are born with a coat like that of the adult,
the primary white coat being shed in the uterus. Similarly
a *Cystophora* pup also sheds its grey woolly coat before it
is born and starts life in its elegant 'blueback' coat. Lactation
in phocids and even in the harem holding *Halichoerus* is
much shorter than in otariids and is of the order of 2–4
weeks. The pups of these forms, except of those mentioned
above, shed their primary coats at weaning after which they
are ready to enter the water. The Common Seal gives birth
on sand or mudbanks at low tide[2] and the pup has of
necessity to swim actively at birth or at least a few hours
later unhampered by a long woolly coat. Mating takes place
slightly longer after the birth of the pup than in otariids—
usually from 2–6 weeks after.

No harem formation has been recorded for walruses
although they are said to be polygamous. The pup is fed
by its mother for over a year and it is only gradually during

the second year that it becomes independent. The slow growth of the tusks that are necessary for feeding probably accounts for this long dependence. The young animals stay with their mother for another year and even longer after weaning.

All otariids and phocids so far investigated exhibit delayed implantation of the blastocyst and it is probably a phenomenon common to all species[2, 90, 91]. Only the walrus, judging from the size of the embryos at different times during pregnancy, has blastocysts that implant at the expected time and thus giving a gestation period of almost a full year. Delayed implantation is either related to lactation and an almost immediate post-parturitional ovulation, as in rodents, or is of a much longer duration than lactation and, as in badgers, may last up to two years with blastocysts lying dormant in the uterus. Common Seals mate in late July or early August about six weeks after the pups are born and about the time of, or just after weaning. Evidence from the size of embryos and the lack of pregnant seals in the first three months after mating suggest that the length of delay in this species is from 2–4 months. Various factors influence the length of delay and as some species exhibit out-of-season mating and ovulation not all individuals may display delay in any one year. The precise cause of delayed implantation is not known and although the evidence suggests strongly that there is a hormonal background to the phenomenon, the effects of light, climate and activity cannot be completely excluded. Delayed implantation results in several forms in the birth of pups at almost the same time each year. Fisher[90] points out that the mechanism is not only of ecological significance but essential to the survival of northern forms, such as the Ringed and Harp Seals. Birth in the latter takes place in February and March on northwest Atlantic shores which is the only time when a suitable 'platform' is available in the form of thick pack-ice. Mating is essential soon after birth as that is the only time females are aggregated and available; at other times of the year they are scattered far and wide over an immense area.

It is interesting that at the time the pups take to the sea a surface growth of zooplankton occurs, providing available food at just the right time.

All fur seals, sea lions, walruses, Bearded and Monk Seals have four mammary teats; all other phocids have two. They are retracted beneath the body surface except when in use, concealed in a pit by hair, protected and hardly noticeable. The sheet-like mammary glands are spread out under the blubber over much of the ventral surface of the body and pups may take in up to a gallon of milk at a time. Seal milk, like that of whales, is particularly rich in fat. There is about 45 per cent fat, 10 per cent protein, 45 per cent water, only traces of lactose and a little ash. There is much variation in the composition, depending to some extent on the time in lactation the sample is taken. Human milk contains 3·5 per cent fat, 1 per cent protein, 88·8 per cent water and 6·5 per cent lactose. The high fat content of seal milk explains why seal pups increase in weight so rapidly, mainly due to deposition of thick blubber. A Grey Seal pup puts on 1·5 kg a day during the time it sucks and the mother loses over 2·5 kg a day during the same period. Southern Elephant Seal pups gain 9·0 kg a day and during lactation the cow may lose as much as 300 kg.

The thyroid gland[2, 80] in the Common Seal exhibits two periods of maximum activity. One of these occurs in the adult seal during lactation and there is a well-known connection between thyroid activity, lactation and the fat content of milk. The pituitary of the pup is precociously developed at birth compared to that of terrestrial carnivores and it is thought to be correlated with an adaptation in water metabolism needed to deal with such concentrated milk. This enlargement and activity of the pup's pituitary and the second period of thyroid maximal activity which occurs in late foetal life may have some connection with the precocious enlargement of the foetal gonads[2, 80, 91]. There is an increased amount of interstitial tissue and blood vessels in the gonads of late foetal and newborn phocids so that both ovaries and testes are almost the same size as those of adult seals. These organs have diminished considerably in size by a fortnight after birth. There is also a related stimulation of prostatic activity in such pups and occasionally of the uterus masculinus. The uterine mucosa is also stimulated, but the pup's mammary glands appear unaffected. This stimulation of the late foetal and newborn gonads and secondary reproductive organs appears hormonal in origin, but the source of these hormones could be the maternal endocrines, the placenta, the foetal pituitary or possibly some combination of all three[80].

A single annual pup is normal to most seals although twin foetuses have been recorded. A small proportion of mature females do not become pregnant every year, particularly in walruses of which only about half the females pup in any one year. Bearded Seals and possibly Laysan Monk Seals as well produce young only every second year. There have been occasional intergeneric matings reported in animals in captivity. Several have occurred between Grey and Ringed Seals but the pups have always been born dead. A female *Zalophus* mated with a male South African Fur Seal produced three pups in successive years; two of them died within a day but the third, a male, lived for about 6 months and was said to resemble its father.

The ovaries[2,91] are enclosed in a bursa which is often found to contain fluid, especially in oestrus. The surface of the organ is indented by a series of crypts lined by covering epithelium. These subsurface crypts become more marked and complex during the breeding season, and may communicate with cyst-like spaces in the ovarian cortex. They are present in other carnivores and are particularly marked in badger ovaries. Usually only one follicle matures during each oestrous period. Follicular enlargement in fact starts in late pregnancy though several become atretic: one persists into the post-parturitional period and is the one that ovulates in oestrus. It is usually stated that ovulation is induced by mating but there is some evidence from seals kept in captivity that it can be spontaneous. There is definite evidence[90] of spring ovulations in Common and

Grey Seals and out-of-season ovulation and mating may well occur in other species though it is probably only younger females, that have not established the true reproductive pattern of the species, which display it. There has been some discussion as to when pinnipeds reach sexual maturity and it probably occurs later than is generally recognized. Common Seals do not ovulate until their third or fourth year and bulls do not reach sexual maturity until later, possibly not until their sixth year[80]. The corpus luteum usually persists until term though it often shows evidence of degeneration. It usually enlarges during lactation showing some evidence of post-parturient rejuvenation as in the cat. It starts to degenerate and to be invaded by connective tissue soon after parturition and by 6 weeks has shrunk to a small corpus albicans. It soon disappears altogether and counting of the scars of old corpora is no use as a method of ageing seals as it is in some cetaceans (p. 93).

The bicornuate uterus has a dividing septum in its fused part that is incomplete caudally in phocids so that the rather smaller common chamber leads by a single opening into the vagina. The septum is longer in otariids and walrus and may divide the entire fused part of the uterus so that there are two openings into the vagina. The cyclical changes in the uterine mucosa are not dissimilar to those in terrestrial carnivores except that during the period of delay in implantation the mucosa enters a resting stage and only the cells lining the uterus show evidence of secretion. A small os clitoris has been found in many seals. The anus and urogenital canal open into a common cloaca surrounded by a sphincter muscle. The vagina[91] is simple and lacks the folds found in cetaceans; its epithelium is stratified squamous during most of the reproductive cycle but shows changes during delayed implantation and late pregnancy.

The testes are inguinal in phocids and walrus, internal to the blubber, and showing no external indication of their presence. This position is reached some months before birth. Care should be taken by anyone first dissecting a phocid seal for the testes to avoid confusing them with the

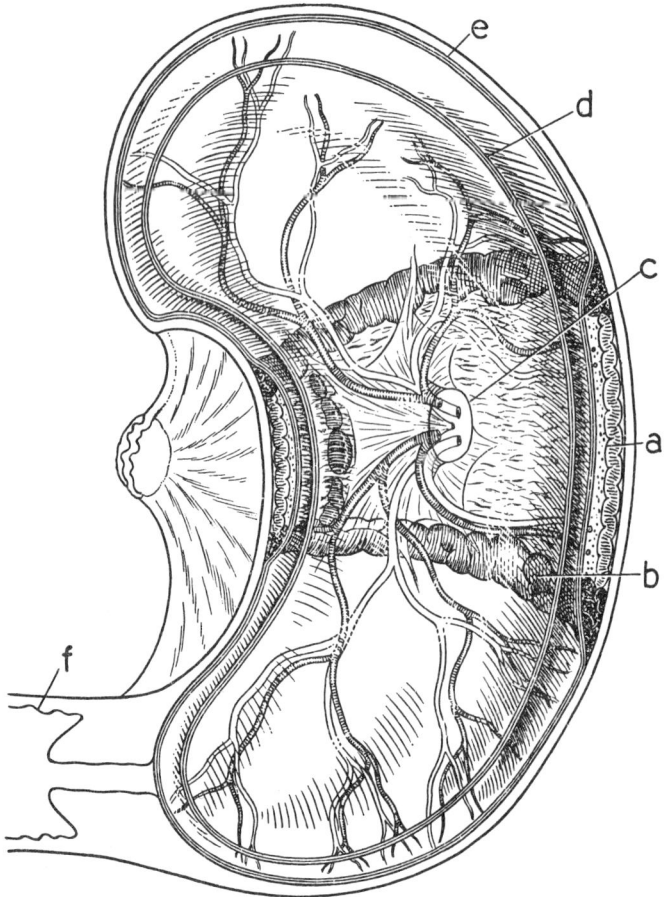

Fig. 9. Seal placenta. Diagram of the chorio-allantoic placental band
and foetal membranes in a Common Seal
 a Zonary placental band (chorio-allantoic placenta)
 b Marginal 'haematoma'
 c Umbilical cord and vessels (cut)
 d Amnion and allantois
 e Chorion and allantois
 f Vagina

large lymphatic nodes in the inguinal region. In otariids the testes are scrotal, covered with black naked skin and do not descend there until the third or fourth year. The testes of all seals so far examined[91] display a seasonal activity and spermatozoa are stored in the epididymis as in other mammals. The penis is retracted within a cutaneous pouch and there is a well-developed os penis or baculum that increases in size throughout life. The size of the bone can provide evidence of the age of a male seal. Mating usually occurs on land, or on ice floes, or in shallow water at the edge of the shore or beach.

There are few observations on early stages in placentation in pinnipeds and although it is known that there is a yolk-sac or choriovitelline placenta present during the early months details are lacking. It would appear to atrophy after a few months though traces of it can be found in the full-term placenta. The chorio-allantoic placenta[2] is large and zonary in the form of a band surrounding the middle of the foetus (Fig. 9). It is usually incomplete at the point where the choriovitelline placenta had contact with the maternal tissues. Beyond the annular band the membranous chorion projects caudally and cranially to enclose the foetal head and tail. The allantois is very large and almost completely surrounds the amnion. The umbilical cord contains two arteries and two veins all of which divide to spread out over the mesometrial aspect of the placental band and also on to the membranous chorion. The placental band is laby-rinthine in its construction with large, dilated maternal sinusoids lined by an irregularly thickened endothelium. The trophoblast of the chorionic plates in the labyrinth is separated from the maternal endothelium by a thick layer of perivascular substance that is of particular interest in any carnivore placenta. The origin of this substance has been the subject of much enquiry and electron microscopy of the layer in the Common and Grey Seal placenta suggests that it is no inert structure and that it must play an important part in certain aspects of placental transfer. The relationship of foetal and maternal tissues is thus endotheliochorial from the standpoint of the Grosser-Mossman classification. In those pinniped placentae that have been examined the barrier between the foetal and maternal circulations is strikingly thin. It is less than $1 \cdot 0$ μ thick in many places and much of its thickness is provided in full-term placentae by the perivascular substance. It is not impossible that the thinness of the intervening barrier is an adaptation related to facilitating gaseous exchange to a foetus that is in danger of becoming anoxic if the mother dives with a slowed heart rate (p. 135). It is not known whether the foetal heart rate also slows during a dive, but it is known that a near-term foetus is able to display the diving bradycardia when removed from the uterus of a dead cow. The thin placental barrier may also allow maternal hormones to pass easily to the foetus and thus produce the changes in the foetal gonads described on p. 143.

The lobulated marginal region of the placental band is brightly coloured from a pink tinge to a dark red-brown[2]. This zone has been called a 'marginal haematoma' in other placentae, especially that of dogs. Similar regions are also found in other places on the placental band in seals and show variations in complexity of structure and in size. The 'haematomata' are not really correctly named; they contain cell debris, bilirubin and cholesterol esters and are lined with chorionic trophoblast which also projects into the internal spaces in villus-like tufts. The trophoblast is here composed of tall columnar cells with microvilli on their free surfaces. The cells contain phagocytosed maternal red cells in various stages of destruction and degradation. The maternal cells have entered the 'haematomata' as the result of rupture of maternal sinusoids although there does not seem to be any proper circulation passing through these marginal regions. In both fissiped and pinniped carnivores these regions are important as sites of iron transfer to the foetus, as a result of breaking down of maternal red cells. They are particularly important to seals for even their foetuses have a high blood volume (p. 133) and high red cell count and presumably a high demand for iron. The bilirubin left behind after the red cell destruction is not lost if the cow eats the placenta after birth of her pup and returns it to be used again in erythropoiesis. This has been observed on a few occasions[71].

The membranous chorion also plays an important part in providing nutriment to the foetus. It effects an epithelio-chorial attachment to the uterine lining and is folded and slightly raised in the regions opposite to the mouths of the uterine glands. These are active throughout pregnancy and secrete material that is absorbed by the trophoblast and passed to the foetus by the allantoic vessels.

7

Manatees and Dugongs

> Every animal doubtless has its appointed place
> and time in the great scheme of creation. Could
> we but for a moment remove that misty film
> which here and there drapes some with tantaliz-
> ing indefiniteness, we should be astonished, and
> bow in reverence to that fiat which has planned
> and carried out such a grand design.
>
> Murie, J. (1872), *On the Form and Structure of
> the Manatee*

Sea cows—manatees and dugongs—are completely aquatic
and live solely on vegetation beneath the water along coasts
and in estuaries and rivers. Besides the two modern groups
mentioned above, a large extinct form, Steller's[142] sea cow
(*Hydrodamalis stelleri*), once inhabited Arctic waters. The
evolutionary history of these curious mammals is not clearly
understood. Simpson[140] coined the new name Paenungulata
(*paene=near*) for a superorder to include them with the
Proboscidea (elephants) and the Hyracoidea (hyraxes),
together with extinct pantodonts and dinocerates. It is
generally accepted that the living forms had a common
proto-ungulate ancestor even if it has yet to be proved.
There was probably not a single primitive phylum that split
into the seven orders placed as paenungulates, but it seems
that there was a protungulate division that developed a
heavy body and other shared characters. The various orders
must have appeared in the Palaeocene, the elephants,
hyraxes and sirenians probably in Africa. Eocene[140] sirenian
fossils (*Protosiren*) are known, with short hind limbs, which
show similarities to the ungulates of the time. The pelvis
was much less specialized, although the skull was essentially
sirenian. These forms were found in the West Indies and

Egypt. Each of the molar tooth crowns in *Desmostylus*, an extinct form from the Miocene of California and Japan, consisted of three parallel rows of cylindrical columns with a single posterior column. There was a large bony rostrum with a pair of long upper tusks curving downwards. Two pairs of smaller lower tusks, the lateral probably the larger, were present in the shovel-shaped lower jaw. It is not impossible that this extinct form was large, quadrupedal, with heavy limbs and that it was semiaquatic.

Steller's[142,143] sea cow (*Hydrodamalis stelleri*) once inhabited the vicinity of Bering and Copper Islands and adjacent regions in the north Pacific. It apparently fed mainly on marine algae but it was exterminated over a hundred and fifty years ago. It was in fact discovered in 1741, when there was a population of only 2,000, and was extinct 27 years later. Steller among many others ate it and declared it like veal. The body had a rough, bark-like skin, and the flippers were said to be covered with short, coarse hairs. The horizontal tail had two laterally pointed lobes. There were seven cervical vertebrae and nasal bones were lacking. Adults were devoid of teeth, horny oral plates being present instead.

The living sea cows[126,131,138] are bulky, elongated creatures, streamlined to some extent but clumsy and lethargic yet precise in their movements. Their appearance is striking in that they lack hind limbs and the tail is flattened and extended into a large horizontal paddle (manatee) or into an almost fluke-like shape (dugong) which lacks any bony support except for the small caudal vertebrae. This, and the fact that they possess thoracic mammary glands, have probably contributed not a little to the origin of the myths about the existence of mermaids or sirens[126]. The snout is short and is like a muzzle. The distinct valvular nostrils are placed on or behind the tip of the dorsal part of the muzzle. Sparsely haired, except for bristles round the mouth, they have a thick epidermis and abundant blubber. The neck region is obscurely marked by a few skin creases and there are others on the ventral part of the abdomen. The forelimbs are large and paddle-like with a pentadactyl pattern of bones; they are mobile and besides being used for equilibration can swish plants towards the mouth when feeding. Clavicles are absent. Swimming is slow and accomplished solely with the tail and hind part of the body. There are twenty or more caudal vertebrae and the associated musculature is well developed. The pelvic girdle is vestigial, giving origin to the penis in the male. There is no true sacrum. The meat is good to eat boiled and tastes like veal cutlet; it is best first washed for a while in cold water. Sadly it was seafaring man's approval of Steller's advice that *Hydrodamalis* was good food, that led to its extinction. A Dr Hobbs, living in Queensland in the last century, recommended the oil obtained by boiling the body fat of dugongs as being therapeutically as good as, if not better than, cod-liver oil. Several thousand manatee hides, and canned meat, were exported from Brazil between 1938 and 1942.

Order SIRENIA
  Suborder TRICHECHIFORMES
    Family Prorastomidae—extinct. Eocene
    Family Protosirenidae—extinct. Eocene
    Family Dugongidae
        Four extinct subfamilies of which the most recent was the Hydrodamalinae (*Hydrodamalis* —Steller's sea cow)
      Subfamily Dugonginae
        Genus *Dugong*—dugong
    Family Trichechidae
        Genus *Trichechus*—manatee
  Suborder DESMOSTYLIFORMES
    Family Desmostylidae—extinct. Upper Oligocene-- Miocene

GENUS TRICHECHUS

Manatees[134,135] are found in rivers and off coasts of Florida to British Guiana (*T. manatus*), in rivers of Brazil[124] (*T.*

inunguis, with no nails on its flippers) and of West Africa (*T. senegalensis*)[126]. They can be recognized by the paddle-like tail (in shape somewhat like that of a beaver), by their dentition and by their having only six cervical vertebrae. Adults reach up to 3 m in length. Skin creases are present behind the head and round the root of the forelimbs and the lumbar part of the trunk. The colour of the body is steel grey to black; the front part of the muzzle, the projecting part of the palate and the lower lips are dull yellow. Anatomists have puzzled over just what the furrowed, bristle-clad, half-moon-shaped upper lip and the strange truncate snout or muzzle resemble (Fig. 10). The position of the external nares on the top of the snout hardly helps in making an assessment. Murie[135] concluded, not in our opinion correctly, that it is like an elephant's trunk that had contracted very considerably with loss of the tactile part. Whatever its homology, the expanded upper lip is most efficient in cropping vegetation[124].

The wide, deep, truncate end to the manatee snout, and in particular the remarkable mobility of the lips, make this part of the animal difficult to describe. The sides of the upper lip in a relaxed animal overhang the lower one like the pendulous upper lips of a bloodhound. Viewed from in front the anterior corners of the upper lip, the lip pads, hang down lower than the central portion and it is these lip pads that can be approximated to one another and used for manipulating vegetation into the mouth. The mobile upper lip is well developed and loosely connected to the bone. The sparse, soft hairs on the head increase in number towards the rounded end of the snout and are continued on the inner side of the upper lip as far as the dental plate and on the inner sides of the cheeks as far back as the teeth. The skin of the inner cheeks is grey like that on the external surface. On the inner sides of the depending, mobile lip pads are two smallish areas of stiff bristles, like small tooth-brushes, that convey the food and there are a few bristles on the outer surface of the lips.

The anterior upper edge of the lower lip is a sharp-edged

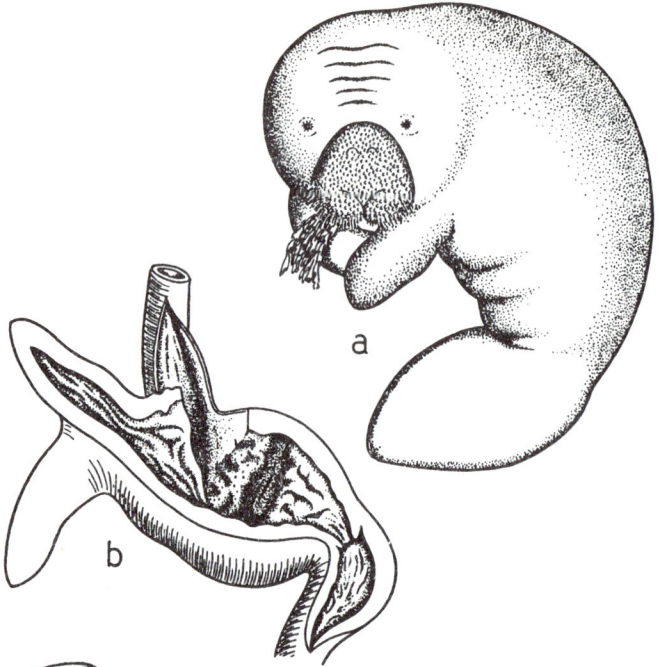

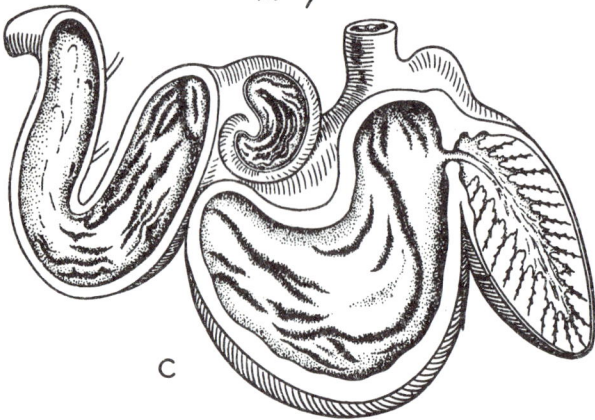

a

b

c

semicircular rim and between this and the dental plate, on what would normally be the inner surface of the upper lip, the skin is grey and studded with bristles. Soft hairs are present on the skin along the sides of the dental plate.

Within the mouth anterior to the teeth and lying on the symphyseal areas of the premaxillae and lower jaw are the hardened, horny dental plates, not unlike the single upper dental plate of a cow or sheep. They are covered with rough, horny, conical papillae and soft filiform papillae. The tongue is bound down at its base and cannot be protruded; there are numerous papillae on its surface. The salivary glands are strikingly large, particularly the parotids.

There is a well-developed third eyelid, a nictitating membrane at the medial aspect of the eye. A cartilage is attached to it, as in elephants. There is no lacrimal gland, nor nasolacrimal duct. The eye is very small compared with the size of the orbital cavity; it has some fat and a marked retial mass round it, and below the thick bundle of infraorbital nerves that innervates the upper lip and its appendages. The sclera is dense and thick at the back of the eye, as in cetaceans. The pupil is sometimes a transverse oval but in life is usually round[136]. Upper and lower eyelids cannot really be discerned, but there is a series of radiating wrinkles about the palpebral fissure that become twisted together when the eyelids close.

There is no pinna to the ear and the external auditory meatus is very narrow indeed and has even been found to be occluded for part of its S-shaped course. The meatus expands where it reaches the relatively large tympanic membrane. There is no evidence to suggest that the sense of hearing is reduced, it would seem in fact to be acute.

The bodies of the cervical vertebrae are compressed

Fig. 10. Manatee. Stomach and caecum
      a Sketch of a Florida Manatee (*Trichechus manatus*). After Murie[136]
      b The caecum and its appendages in a manatee
      c The stomach and its appendages in a manatee

antero-posteriorly and are very rarely ankylosed (see p. 27). There are 6 cervical (an odontoid process is present on the axis), 17–18 thoracic, never more than 3 sacral (judged sacral from their ligamentous attachments to the ilium) and over 20 caudal vertebrae. It seems likely that it is the third cervical vertebra that has been lost, thus reducing the number from seven. The neural arches are stout but low; posterior to the ribs the tranverse processes are wide, diminishing caudally. Stout median ventral processes (haemapophyses or chevron bones) are present beneath the narrow interarticular cartilages of the caudal vertebrae. The arrangement and diminution of the articular processes in the post-thoracic region gives that part of the spine considerable mobility. The ligamentum flavum between the vertebral laminae is very well developed and markedly elastic. The ribs (17–18) are thick and heavy with a very dense structure; their periosteum continues to deposit bone throughout adult life. It has been suggested that the ribs have a ballast-like action, steadying the animal in the water. The short, unsegmented sternum is elongated and connected by ossified sternal ribs with only the three anterior pairs of vertebral ribs[138].

The scapula has a spine with an elongated and pointed acromion. The tendon of the strong subscapularis muscle pierces and strengthens the shoulder joint. There is little shortening of the limb bones: they are somewhat flattened, the ligaments simple and their joints strikingly loose. The normal five digits are present, the metacarpals increasing in size from the first to the fifth, the latter being somewhat separated from the fourth, an arrangement seen in certain aquatic reptiles. The phalanges are flattened, do not exceed the normal mammalian number, and there may in fact be some reduction, particularly of those of the first digit. The flat leathery external 'paddle' extends up to the elbow, at which joint the forward movement takes place. There is probably no movement at the wrist. The paddles show few creases but are covered on the surface with small wart-like elevations. Rudimentary nails are present at the tips of the second, third and fourth digits (except in *M. inunguis*).

The hip bone is represented only by an irregularly triangular bone with cartilaginous tips: it is quite small (1·5–8·0 cm) and is attached by a suspensory ligament to the transverse process of the third sacral or post thoracic vertebra. The rectus abdominis and the ischio-coccygeus are attached to it. There is no sign of any hind-limb bones.

The vertex of the skull is the densest piece of bone (pachyostosis) we have ever tried to saw, making one wonder at the activity, or lack of it, of the parathyroids. Diploe are virtually absent in the dense bones of the vault. This increase in density of bone is found in other aquatic vertebrates such as mesosaurs, primitive aquatic reptiles.

Fawcett[129] finds that there is a marked lack of osteoclasts in the bones of manatees and thus a suppression of bone resorption. No marrow cavity is formed in either ribs or long bones. There is considerable retardation in endochondral ossification and thus bony maturation is delayed and bones remain relatively short. Perichondral ossification proceeds normally, however, and thus accounts for the thickness of the bones. Lack of osteoclasts means that large amounts of unabsorbed primary bone persist long after it should have been replaced and thus adult bones have resemblances to foetal bones of other mammals. These changes are found in human bones in certain endocrine disorders known as congenital athyroidism and osteopetrosis (Albers-Schonberg disease). It certainly seems relevant that in manatees the thyroid appears histologically to be inactive and in a storage state. Sirenians are also the only marine mammals that eat sea vegetation, some of which contains quantities of iodine. The heavy bones of sirenians could have arisen secondary to an inherent hypothyroidism that developed in an early phase of imperfect adaptation to marine life. Studies on their metabolism have shown that the resting oxygen consumption is much lower in manatees than in all other aquatic mammals and that it is as low as one-ninth that of man under true resting conditions. It is therefore possible that heavy bones, sluggish behaviour and

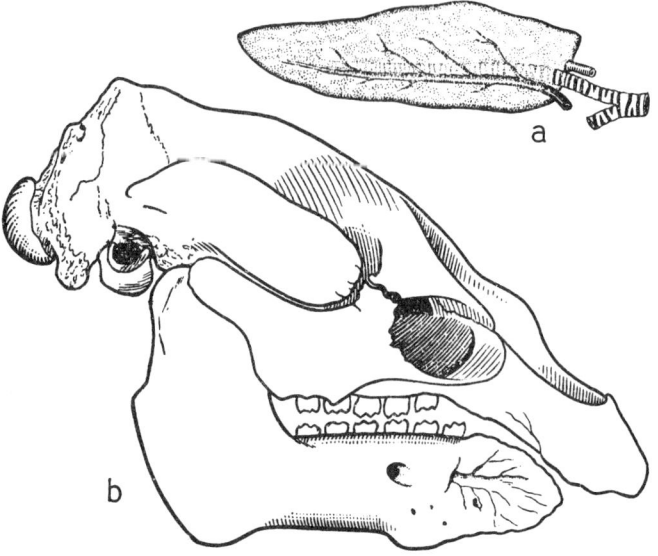

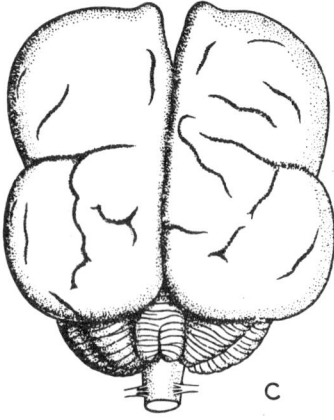

a low metabolic rate are the penalties paid by a mammal that reverts to a marine life, and becomes adapted to eat only sea grasses rather than fish or plankton.

Apart from the sutures on the top of the skull all the other principal sutures are very late in closing and even in an obviously adult skull the temporal bone is remarkably loose in prepared specimens. The cranial cavity is elongated and somewhat cylindrical. The peculiar and characteristic shape of the skull (Fig. 11) is due mainly to the extremely heavy zygomatic arch, the forward position of the orbits, the large narial basin, and the ventral tilting of the pre-maxillae. The great narial basin is perhaps the most obvious feature, its length being almost half that of the skull, and its backward extension having reduced the nasals to a rudimentary condition so that they are not seen in a pre-pared skull. The extension of the bony nares caudally has no obvious connection with the position of the nostrils, which are at the front end of the snout, but is due to the need for more surface area for the attachment of muscles for the complicated lip movements. A similar recession of the posterior margin of the narial basin is also found in the tapir, saiga, Hooded and Elephant Seal, for example, where a mobile proboscis is present. The position of the orbits, anterior to the entire maxillary tooth row, is very unusual. They are roofed over by the frontal, which because of the relative positions of orbits and the posterior end of the narial basin, has to send out two long projections to reach the orbits, and there is a strong post-orbital bar from the jugal which may meet the frontal. The zygomatic pro-cess of the squamosal is particularly deep and thick, and the depth of the entire zygomatic arch is further increased by the large jugal, although the double masseter muscle attached to the arch is not strikingly large. The tympanic

Fig. 11. Manatee skull, brain and lung
    a Lung of a manatee
    b Skull of a manatee
    c Brain of a manatee

bone is like a thickened incomplete hoop. It does not form an inflated bulla, and is fused to the periotic. The mandible is very heavy, the two halves being firmly fused together, and the anterior part of the symphyseal region being flattened and roughened to receive the horny plate. The ascending part is high, and the coronoid process is directed forwards. Surprisingly, the temporalis muscle is relatively small, the large temporal fossa being occupied also by fat and retial tissue.

Only the molar teeth of the manatee erupt and are functional. Two vestigial incisors are present in each jaw at birth but do not erupt through the horny gum pad (this consists of hair-like bodies welded together by epithelium and which serves the incisive function). The molars are all remarkably similar but do increase appreciably in size from the front to the back of the tooth row. They consist essentially of two transversely directed ridges and their crowns are thus approximately bilophodont. The ridges are surmounted by a few small cusps or tubercles when the tooth is newly formed but the identity of these cusps is lost rapidly during functional attrition. There can be no doubt that the more anterior molars have been in function for a longer time; that they are shed by a process involving resorption of their roots when a large amount of attrition has occurred; and that new teeth are continuously being formed in the peculiar alveolar bulb at the posterior end of the tooth row. Dr Alan Boyde reports that in the several adult animals he has examined two unerupted teeth were present in each jaw. The hindermost were at some stage in crown development and the penultimate at some stage in root development. Horizontal succession of teeth occurs as does bone resorption on mesial surfaces and deposition on distal surfaces of the alveoli. The bone supporting the mandibular teeth forms a bridge over the large inferior dental canal and can easily be recognized from the denser, whiter bone of the sides of the alveoli and the body of the mandible. The inferior dental canal is not only large but quite straight and emerges at the mental foramen. It transmits the large complex of nerves and blood vessels which pass straight into the lower lip and are presumably associated with the high mobility and sensitivity of this organ.

The existence of horizontal succession has prevented any reliable estimate being made of the total number of teeth that develop during the life-span of a manatee, if indeed it is limited. There are no reports of animals in which there was no tooth in some stage of development in the alveolar bulb. There would appear to be four to seven teeth erupted in each quadrant at any one time and estimates of as many as twenty successional teeth in each quadrant have been made.

The prisms of the enamel of both manatees and dugongs are remarkably straight and parallel with one another. This characteristic absence of prism decussation is shared by odontocetes, some Insectivora and some Chiroptera. The enamel prisms of sirenians, odontocetes and the same members of the Insectivora and Chiroptera also share the common feature that they are round, separated by abundant interprismatic substance and are usually encircled by complete prism-sheaths. It has often been stated that vascular canals are present near the periphery of the orthodentine of the manatee and that a central axis of vasodentine exists in dugong molars. Recent investigation (Boyde, unpublished) has, however, revealed no signs of this peculiarity. Similar canals in the teeth of other forms may well be post-mortem fungal 'bore-holes'. The so-called vascular channels in manatee dentine may well be simply prominent interglobular spaces.

Many authorities have commented on the interesting features of the panniculus carnosus muscle[8,138]. The main mass stretches from the pelvic region to as far forward as below the eye and is in places as much as 4·0 cm thick. It is a broad, powerful sheet sending some fibres to the fore-limb whilst others pass beneath the neck to form a sphincter colli. It helps strengthen the abdomen and acts as a substitute for the missing costal cartilages. It also plays an important part in swimming, together with the rectus

6

abdominis. The muscles of one side acting alone produce a twisting movement of the body; acting together they depress the tail.

There is a strong cardiac sphincter at the lower end of the muscular oesophagus which contains many mucous glands in its walls. The stomach has an interesting structure (Fig. 10): the main compartment is shaped like a human stomach, but there is occasionally a protuberant left-sided retro-oesophageal recess just cranial to the entrance of a distinct, knob-like cardiac gland about 8 cm long and nearly as broad. This gland feels very firm and is almost solid with complex, internal foliate folds. The lining mucous membrane is thick and full of gastric glands containing enormous numbers of oxyntic (acid producing) cells. It seems that although the true gastric mucosa also contains oxyntic cells the animal has evolved an organ capable of providing additional gastric secretion. The main chamber has few rugae and leads through a strong pyloric sphincter into a dilated duodenum with longitudinal folds in its walls. Two appendages or caeca are present at the pyloric end of the main chamber. They are coiled, their walls exhibit longitudinal furrows and they open into the duodenum beyond the pylorus. The lining mucous membrane of the caeca is of the gastric type with both oxyntic and peptic cells. The bile duct and pancreatic ducts open separately into the duodenum. A large gall bladder is present.

The small intestine is very muscular and in a 2·5 m male we examined is over 8 m in length. It lacks villi and crypts: the lining of the intestine .is also interesting in that the epithelium is not a single layer of columnar cells but consists of two layers of low squamous cells. There is a powerful ileo-caecal sphincter, a caecum and two conical caecal appendages (Fig. 10). The large intestine lies peripheral to the small intestine within the abdomen and is over 6 m in length. There are no taeniae coli. There are many mucous glands in its lining, which also has a stratified superficial layer of squamous epithelial cells instead of the columnar cells found in other mammals. This striking modification of the intestinal lining is possibly related to the need to restrict water absorption. It may also be related to the structure of the manatee kidney, in that without the lobulated form as found in pinnipeds and cetaceans, it is unable to clear large amounts of water.

The diaphragm is thin and is placed almost horizontally in the animal. It stretches from the very short sternum about the level of T4 down to the last ribs and separates the surprisingly small, flattened, elongated lungs in the dorsal compartment from the abdominal viscera lying ventrally.

The epiglottis is rudimentary, unlike that of the cetacean, and the vocal cords are replaced by fleshy and prominent cushions. The trachea divides some 15 cm cranial to the lungs and the bronchi lie parallel and bound together for some 8 cm until they part to enter almost at the summit of the lung. There are eight to twelve tracheal rings, several being bifurcate. The lungs[144] appear symmetrical (Fig. 11). Each main stem bronchus extends straight to the caudal extremity of the lungs on its medial aspect immediately beneath the visceral pleura. Some twelve secondary bronchi leave the main stem and pass laterally into the lung substance. There is no lobulation of the lung and few notches on its borders. The air sacs are very large, and correspond to the alveolar ducts and saccules of terrestrial mammals. The large alveolae branch from them with dilated mouths.

There are several interesting features in the vascular system[94], some having an undoubted functional significance[6,128]. The most striking are the retia: they are in the form of vascular bundles rather than networks. A main artery and its *vena comitans* break up into more or less parallel small arteries and thin-walled veins either freely intertwined or with a regular pattern. The vessels lie enclosed in loose connective tissue and the whole complex is enclosed within a strong fibrous sheath. In the caudal rete of *Trichechus* the main artery divides proximally, one division breaking up into the vascular bundle, while the other continues distally, unchanged, within the bundle.

These bundles are found in the face and jaw region, limbs, body and thoracic walls and spinal canal, as well as in the caudal region. The possible functions of these retial bundles are discussed on p. 71.

The heart is large, globular and exhibits a large interventricular cleft. There are two superior venae cavae. The two pulmonary veins unite to enter the left atrium by a single opening. The abdominal vena cava is duplicated and a small hepatic sinus is present. There is no distinct caval sphincter, but we have found a thin band of diaphragmatic muscle passing round the vena cava from the ventral aspect of the diaphragm in the form of a muscular sling reminiscent of that found in *Zalophus* and *Phocoena*. It would not seem to be particularly effective in occluding the venous return to the heart. In view of the discussion on p. 135, and as there is little doubt that manatees are not able to dive for prolonged periods, it seems unlikely that these features are necessarily associated with a diving bradycardia[94]. The heart rate is said to be between fifty and sixty beats a minute. There is, however, a pair of extradural intravertebral veins ventral to the spinal cord and surrounded by retial tissue. They are best developed in the thoracic region but even there they are not as large relatively as in some other aquatic mammals.

The kidney[127] is simple with only a superficial indication of any lobulation. There is no stellate plexus of veins on the surface and the renal vein leaves the hilus in the usual mammalian manner. The testes are abdominal and there are large seminal vesicles. The penis projects through the prepuce on the anterior abdominal wall half-way between the anus and the umbilicus. The 'prostate' is not glandular but is composed of erectile muscular tissue.

Several features of the nervous system of sirenians have caused surprise and comment[127,131,138]. Elliot Smith wrote: 'Among the whole series of placental mammals there is no other animal in which the brain presents features so extraordinary and bizarre as in the Sirenia. The only parallel which can be found for the peculiar cases presented by the manatee and the dugong is that occasionally presented in the brains of idiots, in which the process of elaboration has ceased in the earlier months of intrauterine life, and the organ has simply grown in size without becoming perfected in structure'.

One is immediately struck by the overall impression of a foetal-like brain because of the relatively few sulci (Fig. 11) and their shallowness, and by the thinness of the lepto-meninges. The brain weight in adults is about 300 g. The outline of the brain, seen from above is quadrangular with rounded corners: the height, breadth and length are almost equal. The posterior cerebral lobe hardly covers half the cerebellum. The hemispheres are divided by a deep, wide longitudinal fissure and there is a deep transverse Sylvian fissure which does not always reach to the medial surface of the hemisphere. The anterior aspect of the frontal lobe is almost vertical and the well developed olfactory nerve and bulb are found in the middle of its lower part. There is some evidence from observing animals in captivity to suggest that the sense of smell is good. The fornix is well developed. The occipital lobe is broadened at the back and concave laterally below to cover the large para-floccular lobe of the cerebellum. The corpus callosum is short but thick; the anterior commissure is small. Both the corpus striatum and the thalamus are large. The optic nerve is slender and the chiasma lies as a transverse ridge on the base of the brain. The ventricles are capacious, but the posterior horn is reduced or absent. Unlike cetaceans manatees cannot be taught tricks.

Manatees are seldom seen in groups but large aggregations form during cold spells in tropical waters, such as those of the Everglades National Park in Florida, where there is no special warming feature in evidence to attract them[135]. Groups also collect in such places as the relatively warm outflow of a giant spring. Each manatee may have an independent range; however much of it overlaps that of others, and its only occasional attendance at aggregation points shows a remarkable independence of behaviour.

There is some suggestion of seasonal migration, but not necessarily by every individual.

A manatee aggregation is very quiet during the cold early morning and animals show little more than their snouts above water. As the sun warms the water the manatees expose more of their bodies and stay longer at the surface. They rise and sink effortlessly and, if the aggregation is dense, often bump into another above. If it is the face that is bumped, Moore states that there is a 'nuzzling of the presented body surface for a moment in a mildly interested, exploratory manner'. When adults predominate their 'usually mild movement is occasionally intensified into a violent, thumping swirl', probably an expression of emotional release. Adults lying close and rising to breathe together sometimes placed their snouts in contact, first below the water, then above water as if indulging in a form of kissing which is probably a gesture of greeting or identification. The length of time spent below water has been given as 7–16 minutes[139]; personal observations suggest that in young, about half-grown, manatees the longest dives seldom exceeds 8 minutes and most dives are less than 5 minutes. It is, however, long enough for an animal to sink and move off under water for thirty or more metres before surfacing for the next breath. Manatees usually dive with the lungs full of air[139] and have not been observed to exhale under water as a dive progresses. Moore[135], incidentally, observes that manatees can use their flippers to scull themselves slowly to right or left, and that when swimming against the current could use them in alternate antero-posterior strokes to aid the tail movements. There are statements in the literature that the tail can be used for backing under water and even heaving a manatee backwards into the water when its front half is out on a bank. Captive animals have been seen walking in shallow water on the inturned tips of their flippers but almost everyone seems to be convinced that adult manatees are quite incapable of locomotion when completely stranded. When quite out of water they are unable to breathe properly because of the weight of their bodies and try to turn on to their backs.

Little is known about reproduction in sirenians[2]. Evidence presented by Moore suggests that breeding occurs in manatees every other year, that there is no distinct breeding season, that there is usually only one calf at a time and that it can be born in any month of the year. Gestation lasts a year. The young stay with the mother for two years and reach full size after four. Moore[135] has also disposed of the legend that the cow suckles her young in a vertical position with it embraced by her flipper and its head above water. This legend accounts for the origin of the name manatee, given it by Spanish colonists in the West Indies (manati or manattoui—*mano*, hand; *tener*, to hold). Suckling in fact takes place in a horizontal position, under water and without any embracing. The cow extends her flipper laterally and forwards, the calf lies at an angle to her body and sucks at the pectoral nipple either with its snout above water or under it as the pair sink.

There are few descriptions of placentation in sirenians and early accounts are not altogether reliable. Wislocki[146] states that the chorioallantoic placenta of a 44 cm foetus of *T. manatus* is zonary and strictly delimited although it is possible that it is diffuse in early stages (Fig. 12). No yolk sac has been seen. The allantois is large, filling the chorionic sac except for a small area where the amnion fuses with the chorion. The amnion is covered with minute elevations or plaques of epithelial cells. The umbilical cord breaks into four leashes of vessels that fan out along the zonary placental band and also out onto the well vascularized membranous chorion. The allantois is reflected about the four main divisions of the cord vessels so that its cavity is divided into four main compartments, the two median ones being the smaller.

The adventitial sheaths of the placental vessels where they cross the surface of the band are thickened in numerous places to produce white protuberances. These have a waxy appearance, are often arranged in rows and sometimes form

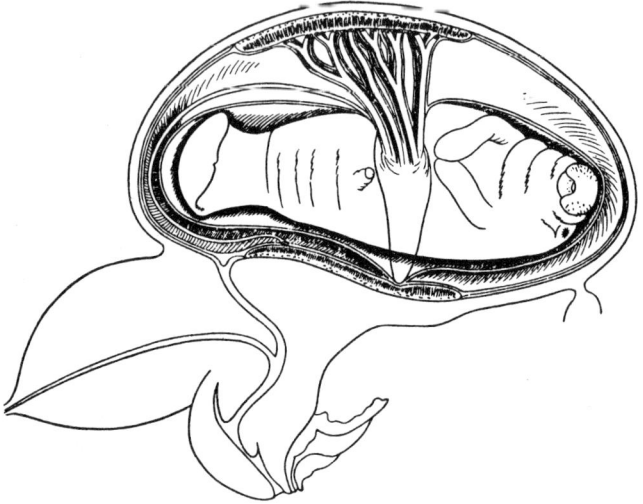

Fig. 12. Manatee uterus and placenta
Diagram of a pregnant uterus of a manatee. After Wislocki[145]

cauliflower-like masses on stalks. They often arise singly
from the surface of the placental tissue unrelated to blood
vessels. At most some 4 mm in diameter, they are due to a
proliferative growth of the allantoic mesoderm. In this
respect, as well as in many features already described, the
placenta of the manatee resembles that of an elephant.
The placental band is made up of intimately fused lobes of
variable size and contour, 4 to 8 cm in diameter. In a cross
section several zones can be discerned in the labyrinthine
structure of the band. At the surface there is a zone consisting of arcades of columnar trophoblast enclosing spaces
into which maternal blood has escaped and stagnated.
Maternal red cells are phagocytosed there by the trophoblast. The superficial region of the labyrinth is thus much
more darkly coloured than the deeper regions. These consist of more or less marked trabeculae of trophoblast
arranged vertically about the streams of maternal blood.
Foetal capillaries are profusely arranged within the trabeculae. The relationship between the two blood streams in
this part of the labyrinth is haemochorial. At the base of
the labyrinth tongues of syncytial trophoblast penetrate the
uterine mucosa and push out along the walls of maternal
vessels. The walls of these vessels undergo attrition and
their rupture leads to maternal blood circulating freely
through the interstices of the labyrinth.

The membranous chorion, i.e. that part of the chorion on
each side of the zonary band, is closely applied to the
intact uterine epithelium but does not appear to be fused
with it. About a dozen accessory placental areas, although
only a few millimetres in diameter, reproduce the structure
of the main band.

GENUS DUGONG

Dugongs (the word is Malayan) are exclusively marine[126].
Although never coming out on land they stay near the coast
where sea grasses are most easily available. *D. dugon* is
seldom over 2·4 m long and lives in the Indian Ocean from

the east coast of Africa to the Malayan Archipelago, and to northern Australia, where fair numbers exist on the east and north coasts of Queensland[130], in the Gulf of Carpentaria, and in Torres Strait. Dugongs are edible and indeed palatable. The therapeutic and culinary qualities of the oil led to extensive commercial exploitation of the Australian dugong in the nineteenth century. It is also eaten by Muslims who are forbidden to eat pig but can eat dugong, which in Tamil and Sinhalese means 'sea-pig'.

They can be distinguished from the manatees[8] by the shape of the tail, the position of the nostrils, their tusks and cheek teeth, the well-developed rostrum, the lack of a post-orbital bar, the presence of seven cervical vertebrae, the short acromion and by a number of characteristics in other parts of their structure. The nostrils of manatees and dugongs are similar, forwardly directed, paired and crescentic 'as if a thumb had been pressed into the skin'. In manatees they are on the tip of the snout, but in dugongs, because of the larger rostrum, they are farther back. Dugongs resemble manatees in many ways, but are usually regarded as being more specialized in that they have lost all traces of nails, because of the shape of the tail and features in the brain and also on odontological grounds.

In overall shape dugongs resemble manatees[131], but are perhaps better streamlined, lacking pronounced skin creases and having a quite differently shaped tail. It has a crescentic notch at the back and is expanded laterally into quite sharp tips so that it much resembles a cetacean fluke. There is a smooth dorsal surface to the muzzle, markedly curved from side to side and on which the closely set valvular external nostrils are set in the midline[138]. The dorsal surface is separated from the forward and somewhat downward facing surface by a crescentic border. This facial surface is flat with a horseshoe-shaped indentation where the centre of the upper lip might be considered to be, and with deeper clefts to each side of it, lateral to which the outer rounded parts of the muzzle hang down like firm jowls on the sides of the mouth. It is covered with large bristles and smaller stiff hairs; these are most plentiful on the lower part of the muzzle and are used for scratching off vegetation and guiding it towards the mouth. The latter is narrow and guarded above by the dilated upper gum with its covering of horny epithelium. The lower lip bears a few large spines and some stiff hairs: the lower jaw has a horny pad covering the anterior down-turned part of the mandible. The hard palate has an anterior rugose and a posterior tuberculated region. The tongue cannot be protruded: it is covered with large filiform papillae. The large parotids appear to be the only salivary glands.

The skull[141] shows great development of the premaxillae into a downward-bent rostrum and a corresponding elongation downwards of the symphyseal region of the mandible. The recession of the narial opening with the lack of nasals, and the position of the orbit, are approximately as in manatees, but the zygomatic arch is not so deep. The male has a pair of upper, modified incisors which are deeply embedded in their premaxillary alveolae and whose tips protrude only slightly into the mouth. They in fact hardly protrude beyond the upper lip and should not really be called tusks. They do not erupt at all in females, yet there is no difference between the size of the 'tusks' in the two sexes. They are described as subtrihedral and have almost the same diameter from base to apex. They seem to be worn away predominantly on their labial aspect, perhaps by friction against the upper lip. They are thus bevelled on the opposite face to that of the chisel-shaped incisors of rodents.

There are also two abortive upper central incisors and many vestigial teeth in the anterior region of the mandible. These teeth never erupt but the tissue in the depressions may help anchor the dental plate. The molars are cylindrical teeth[133] and possess a number of small cusps or tubercles when first formed but these are soon worn away in function. They are usually grooved on both buccal and lingual aspects. They are said to grow from 'semi-persistent' pulps for some time after eruption. Some degree of horizontal succession occurs. A total of six molars in each quadrant is usually described but the earlier erupting anterior teeth are often shed before the last molar comes into occlusion. They are said to lack enamel as adults, though it may be present on the tips of both incisors and molars in young animals, and the bulk of each molar tooth is made of orthodentine and cementum. The presence of vasodentine in sirenians has been maintained in the past but it would seem that there are other explanations for such appearances (p. 161).

The skeleton is in most respects similar to that of the manatee. There are seven cervical vertebrae, the ribs are less thick and heavy, the scapula has a short acromion, but well-developed coracoid, the tuberosities on the humerus are prominent, and there is a tendency for the fusion of some carpals.

The brain is more elongated than that of the manatee and the cerebral hemispheres even more widely separated by the median longitudinal fissure. There is a pseudo-sylvian sulcus separating the smaller rounded frontal lobe from what may be considered an undivided temporo-parieto-occipital lobe. A shallow Sylvian fossa is present at the lower part of the lateral surface and the insular cortex forms a bridge connecting the inferior part of the frontal with what represents the temporal lobe. A few shallow sulci are present on the frontal, parietal and temporal lobes. A single sulcus is present on the medial aspect of the hemisphere and is probably a combined calcarine and calloso-marginal. Both the pulvinar of the thalamus and the lateral geniculate body may be seen from below. The olfactory lobe and stalk are long and cylindrical and, opposed to the manatee, lie far apart on the orbital surface of the frontal lobe. The small optic tracts lie almost transversely across the base of the brain. There are no mammillary bodies. The cerebral peduncles are large and flattened and there is a large interpeduncular body. There is no pineal, but a large habenular apparatus is present. The corpus callosum is well developed and as in manatees the ventricles are large.

The corpora quadrigemina, especially the inferior, are

prominent, again suggesting perhaps that auditory responses are not lacking. The pons is well marked but transverse, with large trigeminal roots leaving it laterally. Behind it is a very distinct trapezoid body leading laterally to the roots of the facial and stato-acoustic nerves. There is some evidence to suggest that vestibular fibres are abundant. The cerebellum is well developed and possesses large floccular lobes composed mainly of the paraflocculus, probably again associated with pronounced swimming and equilibratory activities.

In the buccal cavity, near the origin of the palatoglossal fold, there is a curious, short, stout projection of horny material directed backwards and medially. Owen considered it an outgrowth of the tongue but it would seem more likely to be of pharyngeal origin. Tonsils appear to be lacking. The soft palate is long and smooth and the epiglottis is poorly developed. The viscera show many resemblances to those of the manatee[132]. The stomach has much the same features, possessing two pyloric caeca but the caecal gland is not a conical projection, rather a glandular body in the submucosal layer. The great omentum is small, devoid of fat, is not connected with the colon or its mesentery and appears distinctly embryonic in its arrangement. The lesser sac of peritoneum is virtually closed off from the greater. The small intestine is long, thick walled and muscular. The large intestine is thinner and there is a caecum but with only one caecal appendage. There is a distinct mesentery to the colon. In the anal canal longitudinal columns end in globular swellings acting as anal valves.

The liver[138] has three main lobes and is flattened against the almost horizontal diaphragm. A fourth, Spigelian, lobe lies on the dorsal aspect and is firmly adherent to the posterior vena cava. There is no hepatic sinus, the hepatic veins are not especially dilated and no trace has been found of a caval sphincter. The gall bladder is small and lies on the ventral aspect of the central hepatic lobe. The common bile duct has a long course before opening into the duodenum usually together with the pancreatic duct.

There are no true vocal cords but there are cushion-like protuberances as in manatees. The trachea is very short, with only four cartilaginous rings and is almost completely subdivided by a mid-line septum. The bronchi are long and are said to have spiral cartilages. The lungs are not lobulated, are devoid of fissures and notches and remarkably symmetrical. As in manatees the hilum of the lung is at its apex. Only the pulmonary artery enters the lung substance at the hilum, the bronchus and pulmonary vein passing downwards on the ventro-medial aspect almost to the caudal extremity. The bronchial cartilages extend to the periphery of the lung and are found on the smallest bronchioles. The air sacs are relatively large and there is much elastic tissue.

The vascular system appears to have much the same characteristics as in manatees[2]. The heart and great vessels have a similar appearance, the abdominal posterior vena cava is duplicated and retial vascular bundles are present. Relatively large paired extradural intravertebral veins lie ventral to the spinal cord in the thoracic region: in the cervical region the veins pass dorsal to the cord to enter the skull. Retial tissue also surrounds the cord in this region.

Hill considered the elongated kidneys to be the organs the least mammalian in appearance. They show no superficial lobulation but have a complicated internal structure. There is a large renal sinus within the kidney substance, both cortex and medulla being arranged in ten main pyramids each forming a girdle surrounding the central cavity. This arrangement almost certainly indicates a retained segmentation.

Large seminal vesicles are present and the 'prostate' is like that of the manatee. The prostatic part of the urethra ends in a curious cervix-like projection into the dilated bulbar urethra. The urethra in the female is also surrounded by a prostate-like organ of erectile tissue which also surrounds the caudal part of the vagina. There are certain other interesting features in the female reproductive tract[2].

The ovaries are contained in a bursa, the uterine horns have a characteristic arrangement and structure and the cervical canal appears to become canalized only at puberty. There is also a shield-shaped area of horny material on the ventral wall of the vaginal vault. There is a large conical clitoris and a large triangular urethral caruncle immediately behind it in the vulval cleft[2]. The mammary glands are axillary and the nipples situated almost at the posterior border of the flipper (see p. 167 for comments on suckling position).

Very little is known about reproduction in dugongs, except that one is the usual number of young. The gestation period is a year and it is thought that there is a breeding season restricted to winter months. There is no recent work on the placenta of dugongs. An early description states that the allantois is large, that the chorio-allantoic placenta is at first diffuse, later zonary and that the relationship between foetal and maternal blood streams is epitheliochorial. The material on which these observations were made was poorly preserved and in view of what is known of the manatee's placenta that of the dugong should be examined more thoroughly.

References

A list is given of general works dealing with marine mammals and then follow lists of references in alphabetical order of authors on cetaceans, pinnipeds and sirenians. Space prohibits lists of references for every species and readers are advised to consult those quoted in the general works or reviews marked * for guidance. They should also consult the Zoological Record published by the Zoological Society of London; Reports of the International Whaling Commission, Cambridge; Reports of the Marine Mammal Commission, Washington, D.C.; Special Scientific Reports of the United States Department of the Interior, Fish and Wildlife Service; also special issues of the *J. Fish. Res. Bd. Canada*.

GENERAL WORKS

* 1 Allen, J. A., 1880. *History of North American Pinnipeds*. Washington
* 2 Anderson, H. T., 1969. *The Biology of Marine Mammals*. New York
  3 Delamure, S. L., 1955. *The helminthofauna of marine mammals of the world in the light of their ecology and phylogeny*. (In Russian.) Moscow, 517 pp.
  4 Flower, W. H., 1876. *An introduction to the osteology of the Mammalia*. London
* 5 Gaskin, D. E., 1972. *Whales, Dolphins and Seals*. London and Auckland
* 6 Harrison, R. J., 1972, 1974, 1977. *Functional Anatomy of Marine Mammals*, vols. 1–3. London
* 7 Hershkovitz, P., 1966. *U.S. Nat. Mus. Bull.*, **246.** 1–259. (Living whales, catalogue)
* 8 Howell, A. B., 1930. *Aquatic Mammals*. Baltimore
* 9 King, J. E., 1964. *Seals of the World*. British Museum (Natural History). 2nd ed. 1980

* 10 Matthews, L. H., 1978. *The Natural History of the Whale*. London
* 11 Norman, J. R. and Fraser, F. C., 1948. *Giant Fishes, Whales and Dolphins*. London
* 12 Pilleri, G., 1969–77. *Investigations on Cetacea*. vols. 1–8. Berne
* 13 Ridgway, S. H., 1972. *Mammals of the Sea. Biology and Medicine*. Illinois
* 14 Ronald, K. and Mansfield, A. W., 1975. *The Biology of the Seal. Rapp. P.-v. Réun. Cons. int. Explor. Mer.*, **169**
* 15 Scheffer, V. B., 1958. *Seals, Sea Lions and Walruses*. A review of the Pinnipedia. London
* 16 Slijper, E. J., 1979. *Whales*. 2nd ed. London

CETACEA
17 Alpers, A., 1963. *A Book of Dolphins*. London
18 Breathnach, A. S., 1960. *Biol. Rev.*, **35**, 187–230. (Central nervous system)
19 Cave, A. J. E. and Aumonier, F. J., 1967. *J. roy. microscop. Soc.* **86**, 323–42. (Kidney)
20 Clarke, M. R., 1978. *J. mar. biol. Ass. U.K.,* **58**, 1–17. (Spermaceti organ)
21 de Kock, L. L., 1959. *Acta anat. Basel.*, **36**, 274–92. (Neck arteries and retia)
22 Evans, W. E. and Maderson, P. F. A., 1973. *Am. Zool.*, **13**, 1205–13 (Sound production)
23 Edinger, T., 1955. *Mschr. Psychiat. Neurol.*, **129**, 37–58. (Hearing and smell)
24 Eschricht, D. F., 1886. *Recent Memoirs on the Cetacea*. Ed. W. H. Flower. Ray Society. (*Orcinus*)
25 Essapian, F. S., 1955. *Breviora* (*Mus. Comp. Zool. Harvard*), **43**, 1–4. (Skin folds at speed)
26 Fejer, A. A., and Backus, R. H., 1960. *Nature, Lond.*, **188**, 700–3. (Bow-riding)
27 Fetcher, E. S. and Fetcher, G. W., 1942. *J. cell comp. Physiol.*, **19**, 123. (Kidney)

28 Fraser, F. C., 1934, 1946, 1953, 1974. Reports on Cetacea stranded on the British coasts, no. 11, 1927–32; no. 12, 1933–7; no. 13, 1938–47; no. 14, 1948–66. Brit. Mus. (Nat. Hist.) London

29 Fraser, F. C., 1936. *'Discovery' Rep.*, **14,** 1. (Krill)

30 Fraser, F. C. and Purves, P. E., 1960. *Bull. Brit. Mus. (Nat. Hist.)* **7,** 1–140. (Hearing)

31 Gambell, R., 1976. *Mammal Rev.,* **6,** 41–53. (Whale stocks)

* 32 Harrison, R. J., 1949. *J. Anat. Lond.,* **83,** 238–53. (Reproduction in Pilot Whale)

33 Harrison, R. J. and Ridgway, S. H., 1971. *J. Zool.,* **165,** 355–66. (Reproduction in *Tursiops*)

34 Harrison, R. J., Johnson, F. R. and Young, B. A., 1970. *J. Zool.,* **160,** 377–90. (Stomach)

35 Jacobs, M. S., Morgane, P. J. and McFarland, W. L., 1971. *J. comp. Neurol.,* **141,** 205–72. (Brain)

36 Jansen, N. J., 1950. *J. comp. Neurol.,* **93,** 341–400. (Cerebellum)

37 Jansen, J., 1953. *Hvalrad. Skr.,* **37,** 1–35. (Brain-rhombencephalon)

38 Jonsgård, A., 1966. *Hvalrad. Skr.,* **49,** 1–62. (*Balaenoptera*)

39 Kawamura, A., 1974. *Sci. Rep. Whales. Res. Inst. Tokyo,* **26,** 25–144. (Feeding in Sei Whale)

* 40 Kellogg, R., 1928. *Quart. Rev. Biol.,* **3,** 29 and 174. (History of whales and adaptations)

41 Kellogg, R., 1936. *Carneg. Inst. Wash. Publ.,* **482,** (Archaeoceti)

42 Kellogg, W. N., 1961. *Porpoises and Sonar.* University of Chicago Press

43 Kojima, T., 1951. *Sci. Rep. Whale Res. Inst.,* **6,** 49–72. (Brain of Sperm Whale)

44 Kramer, M. O., 1960. *New Scientist,* **7,** 1118–20. (Locomotion)

45 Lang, T. G., 1966. In *Whales, Dolphins and Porpoises.* Ed. K. S. Norris. Univ. Calif. Press. (Hydrodynamics)

46 Langworthy, O. R., 1932. *J. comp. Neurol.*, **54,** 437–99. (Central nervous system of dolphin)
47 Langworthy, O. R., 1935. *Bull. Johns Hopk. Hosp.*, **57,** 143–7. (Brain of Fin Whale)
48 Laurie, A. H., 1933. *'Discovery' Rep.*, **7,** 363–406. (Respiration)
49 Laws, R. M., 1959. *'Discovery' Rep.,* **29,** 281–308. (Foetal growth weights)
50 Laws, R. M., 1961. *'Discovery' Rep.,* **31,** 327–486. (Fin Whales)
51 Lilly, J. C., 1963. *Science,* **139,** 116–18. (Behaviour of dolphin)
52 Mackintosh, N. A., 1946. *'Discovery' Rep.*, **23,** 177–212. (Antarctic Convergence)
53 Mackintosh, N. A., 1965. *The Stocks of Whales.* London
54 Mackintosh, N. A. and Wheeler, J. F. G., 1929. *'Discovery' Rep.*, **1,** 257–540. (Blue and Fin Whales)
55 Matthews, L. H., 1937. *'Discovery' Rep.*, **17,** 7–92. (Humpback Whale)
56 Matthews, L. H., 1938. *'Discovery' Rep.,* **17,** 169–81. (Sperm Whale)
57 Matthews, L. H., 1948. *J. Anat. Lond.,* **82,** 207–32. (Uterine changes)
58 Miller, G. S., 1923. *Smith. Misc. Coll.,* **76,** 5, 1–72. (Telescoping of skull)
*59 Mitchell, E., 1975. *J. Fish. Res. Board. Can.,* **32** (7), 889–983. (Biology of smaller cetaceans)
60 Ogawa, T., 1935. *Arb. anat. Inst. Send.,* **17,** 63–136. (Brain of seals and whales)
61 Ommanney, F. D., 1932. *'Discovery' Rep.,* **5,** 327. (Retia)
62 Perrin, W. F., 1975. *Bull. Scripps Inst. Oceanogr. Calif.,* **21,** 1–206. (*Stenella*)
63 Purves, P. E., 1963. *Nature, Lond.,* **197,** 334–37. (Locomotion)
64 Purves, P. E. and Mountford, M. D., 1959. *Bull. Brit. Mus.* (*Nat. Hist.*) Zool. **5** (6) (Ear plugs)

65 Rice, D. W. and Wolman, A. A., 1971. *Spec. Publ. Am. Soc. Mammal,* **3,** 1–142. (Grey Whale)

66 Rowlatt, V. and Gaskin, D. E., 1975. *J. Morph.,* **146,** 479–94. (Heart)

67 Ruud, J. T., 1945. *Hvalrad. Skr.,* **23** and **29,** (Age determination from baleen).

68 Scholander, P. F. and Schevill, W. E., 1955. *J. appl. Physiol.,* **8,** 279–82. (Vascular heat exchange in fins)

69 Sergeant, D. E., 1959. *Norsk. Hvalf. Tid.,* **48,** 273. (Age from dentine)

70 Sergeant, D. E., 1973. *J. Fish. Res. Bd. Can.,* **30,** 1065–90. (Beluga)

71 Slijper, E. J., 1956. *Hvalrad Skr.,* **41,** 1–62. (Pregnancy and birth)

72 Slijper, E. J., 1958. *Arch. neerland. Zool.,* **13,** 97–113. (Organ weights)

73 Spoel, S. van der, 1963. *Bijd. Dierk.,* **33,** 71–81. (Renal vessels)

74 Utrecht, W. L. van, 1958. *Zool. Anzeiger,* **161,** 77–82. (Blubber)

75 Walmsley, R., 1938. *Contr. Embryol. Carneg, Instn.,* **27,** 107–78. (Vascular system)

76 Watkins, W. A. and Schevill, W. D., 1974. *J. Mamm.,* **55,** 319–28. (Underwater listening)

77 Wislocki, G. B., 1942. *Anat. Rec.,* **84,** 117–21. (Lung)

78 Wislocki, G. B. and Enders, R. K., 1941. *Amer. J. Anat.,* **68,** 97–126. (Placenta)

PINNIPEDIA

79 Arnason, U., 1974. *Hereditas,* **76,** 179–226. (Chromosomes)

80 Amoroso, E. C., Bourne, G. H., Harrison, R. J., Matthews, L. H., Rowlands, I. W. and Sloper, J. C., 1965. *J. Zool.,* **147,** 430–86. (Reproductive and endocrine organs)

81 Bartholomew, G. A., 1952. *Univ. Calif. Pub. Zool.,* **47** (15), 369–472. (Reproductive behaviour of *Mirounga angustirostris*)

82 Bertram, G. C. L., 1940. *British Graham Land Expedition* 1934–7. *Sci. Rep.* **1** (1), 1–139 (Biology Weddell and Crabeater seals)

83 Blix, A. S., Grau, H. J. and Ronald, K., 1975. *Acta physiol. scand.,* **94,** 133–4. (Brown adipose tissue)

84 Bonner, W. N., 1972. *Oceanogr. Mar. Biol. Ann. Rev,* **10,** 461–507. (Grey and Common Seals)

85 Brooks, J. W., 1954. *Alaska Cooperative Wildlife Research Unit. Spec. Rep.* **1,** 103 pp. (Pacific walrus)

86 Bryden, M. M., 1971. *Antarctic Res. Series Wash.,* **18,** 109–40. (Myology of *Mirounga*)

87 Burne, R. H., 1909. *Proc. Zool. Soc. Lond.,* pp. 732–8. (Walrus anatomy)

88 Denison, D. M. and Kooyman, G. L., 1973. *Resp. Physiol.,* **17** (1), 1–10. (Small airways)

89 Hamilton, J. E., 1934. '*Discovery' Rep.,* **8,** 269–318. (Biology *Otaria byronia*)

90 Harrison, R. J., 1963. In *Delayed Implantation.* Ed. A. C. Enders. Chicago

* 91 Harrison, R. J., Matthews, L. H. and Roberts, J. M., 1952. *Trans. zool. Soc.,* **27,** 437–540. (Reproduction)

92 Harrison, R. J. and Tomlinson, J. D. W., 1956. *Proc. zool. Soc. Lond.,* **126,** 205–33. (Venous system)

93 Harrison, R. J. and Tomlinson, J. D. W., 1960. *Mammalia,* **24,** 386–99. (Diving)

94 Harrison, R. J. and Tomlinson, J. D. W., 1964. In Symp. no. 13 *Zool. Soc. Lond.* (Diving mechanisms)

95 Harrison, R. J. and Ridgway, S. H., 1976. *Deep Diving in Mammals.* Shildon, England

96 Hart, J. S. and Irving, L., 1959. *Canad. J. Zool.,* **37,** 447–57. (Heat regulation in seals)

97 Hiatt, E. P. and Hiatt, R. B., 1942. *J. cell. comp. Physiol.,* **19,** 221. (Kidney function)

98 Howell, A. B., 1928. *Proc. U.S. Nat. Mus.,* **73** (15), 1–142. (Osteology and myology *Zalophus* and *Pusa*)

99 Hubbs, C. L. and Norris, K. S., 1971. *Antarctic Res. Series Wash.,* **18,** 35–52. (Juan Fernandez Fur Seal)

100 Huber, E., 1934. *Carnegie Inst. Wash. Pub. No.* **447,** 105–36. (Facial myology seals and dolphins)

101 Irving, L., 1969. In *The Biology of Marine Mammals.* Ed. H. T. Andersen. Academic Press, New York (Temperature regulation)

102 Kenyon, K. W. and Rice, D. W., 1959. *Pacific Science,* **13,** 215–52. (Life history Hawaiian Monk Seal)

103 King, J. E., 1955. *Bull. Brit. Mus. (Nat. Hist.) Zool.,* **3**.(5), 201–56 (Monk Seals)

104 King, J. E., 1959. *Mammalia, Paris,* **23,** 19–40. (Antarctic Convergence separating two groups of Fur Seals)

105 King, J. E., 1966. *J. Zool.,* **148,** 385–98. (Hooded and Elephant Seals: relationships)

106 King, J. E., 1969. *Brit. Ant. Survey Sci. Rep.,* **63,** 54 pp. (Ross Seal anatomy)

107 King, J. E., 1969. *Austr. J. Zool.,* **17** (5), 841–53. (Fur Seals of Australia)

108 King, J. E., 1977. *J. Zool.,* **181,** 69–94. (Major blood vessels of *Neophoca* and *Phocarctos*)

109 Kooyman, G. L., 1969. *Sci. Am.,* **221** (2) 100–6. (Weddell Seal)

* 110 Laws, R. M., 1953. *Falkland Islands Dependencies Survey Sci. Rep.* 2. (Age determination *M. leonina*)

* 111 Laws, R. M., 1953. *Falkland Islands Dependencies Survey Sci. Rep.* 8. (Growth of Elephant Seal)

* 112 Laws, R. M., 1956. *Falkland Islands Dependencies Survey Sci. Rep.* 13 and 15. (Elephant Seal behaviour and reproduction)

113 Ling, J. K., 1974. In *Functional Anatomy of Marine Mammals.* vol. 2. Ed. R. J. Harrison. Academic Press, London. (Integument)

114 Marlow, B. J., 1975. *Mammalia,* **39** (2), 159–230. (Behaviour of Australasian sea lions)

115 McLaren, I. A., 1960. *Systematic Zoology,* **9,** 18–28. (Pinnipedia biphyletic)

116 Murie, J., 1871. *Trans. zool. Soc. Lond.*, **7**, 411–64. (Anatomy of walrus)

117 Murie, J., 1872 and 1874. *Trans. zool. Soc. Lond.*, **7**, 527–96, **8**, 501–82. (Anatomy *Otaria byronia*)

118 Ray, C. E., 1976. *Syst. Zool.*, **25** (4), 391–406. (Fossil phocids)

119 Repenning, C. A., 1972. In *Functional Anatomy of Marine Mammals*. vol. 1. Ed. R. J. Harrison. Academic Press, London. (Underwater hearing)

120 Repenning, C. A., Petersen, R. S. and Hubbs, C. L., 1971. *Antarctic Res. Series Wash.*, **18**, 1–34. (*Arctocephalus* systematics)

121 Repenning, C. A. and Tedford, R. H., 1977. U.S. Dept. Int. Geol. Survey. Prof. Paper 992, 93 pp. (Fossil otarioids).

122 Shaughnessy, P. D. and Fay, F. H., 1977. *J. Zool.*, **182**, 385–419. (North Pacific Harbour seals)

123 Tedford, R. H., 1976. *Syst. Zool.*, **25** (4), 363–74. (Pinnipeds and carnivores)

SIRENIA

124 Allsopp, W. H. L., 1960. *Nature, Lond.*, **196**, 1329. (Control of vegetation)

125 Beddard, F. E., 1897. *Proc. zool. Soc. Lond.*, 47–53. (Anatomy)

126 Bertram, G. C. L. and Bertram, C. K. R., 1973. *Biol. J. Linn, Soc.*, **5**, 297–338. (Modern Sirenia)

127 Chapman, H. C., 1875. *Proc. Acad. Nat. Sci. Phil.* 452–62. (Anatomy)

128 Fawcett, D. W., 1942. *J. Morph.*, **71**, 105–33. (Vascular system)

129 Fawcett, D. W., 1942. *Amer. J. Anat.*, **71**, 271–309. (Bone)

130 Heinsohn, G. E., and Birch, W. R., 1972. *Mammalia*, **36** (3), 414–22. (Food of dugong)

131 Kaiser, H., 1973. *Morphology of the Sirenia*. Basle

132 Marsh, H., Heinsohn, G. E. and Spain, A. V., 1977.
     In *Functional Anatomy of Marine Mammals*. Ed. R. J.
     Harrison. London. (Dugong stomach)
133 Mitchell, J., 1978. *Zool. J. Linn. Soc.*, **62**, 317–48.
     (Teeth, skull, age of dugong)
134 Moore, J. C., 1951. *J. Mammal*, **32**, 22–36. (Florida
     manatee)
135 Moore, J. C., 1956. *Amer. Mus. Novit. No.* 1811,
     1–24. (Behaviour)
136 Murie, J., 1885. *Trans. zool. Soc. Lond.,* **19**. (Ana-
     tomy)
137 Owen, R., 1839. *Proc. zool. Soc. Lond.,* **28**. (Dugong
     anatomy)
138 Petit, G., 1955. In *Traité de Zoologie, mammiferes.*,
     17, 918–1001. (Anatomy, ethology)
139 Scholander, P. F. and Irving, L., 1941. *J. cell. comp.
     Physiol.*, **17**, 169–91. (Diving)
140 Simpson, G. G., 1932. *Bull. Amer. Mus. nat. Hist.,*
     59, 419–503. (Fossil sirenians)
141 Spain, A. V. and Heinsohn, G. E., 1974. *Austr. J.
     Zool.*, **22**, 249–57. (Dugong skull)
142 Steller, G. W., 1751. *De bestiis marinis*. Novi comm.
     acad. sci. imp. Petropolitanae
143 Stejneger, L., 1887. *Amer. Nat.*, **21**, 1047–54. (Exter-
     mination of *Rytina*)
144 Wislocki, G. B., 1935. *Biol. Bull.,* **68**, 385–96. (Lungs)
145 Wislocki, G. B., 1935. *Mem. Mus. Comp. Zool.
     Harvard*, **54**, 159–78. (Placenta)

Index

Where details of a particular entry are found in the description of each animal the entry is marked with an asterisk, e.g. *Feeding habits, means that the reader should look under the appropriate animal as well as in the main section.